BEYOND COURTS

BEYOND COURTS

A project of
Community Justice Exchange,
Interrupting Criminalization, and
Critical Resistance

Haymarket Books
Chicago, IL

© 2024 Community Justice Exchange, Interrupting Criminalization, and Critical Resistance

Published in 2024 by
Haymarket Books
P.O. Box 180165
Chicago, IL 60618
www.haymarketbooks.org

ISBN: 979-8-88890-313-1

Distributed to the trade in the US through Consortium Book Sales and Distribution (www.cbsd.com) and internationally through Ingram Publisher Services International (www.ingramcontent.com).

This book was published with the generous support of Lannan Foundation, Wallace Action Fund, and Marguerite Casey Foundation.

Special discounts are available for bulk purchases by organizations and institutions. Please email info@haymarketbooks.org for more information.

Cover design by Noah Jodice.

Printed in Canada by union labor.

Library of Congress Cataloging-in-Publication data is available.

10 9 8 7 6 5 4 3 2 1

Contents

About This Book

Beyond Criminal Courts is a collection of resources created for organizers, advocates and community members working together to build the organizing-power we need to defund, divest, and ultimately to dismantle criminal courts for good. Now available in print, *Beyond Criminal Courts* was originally designed as a web-based resource hub. Complete versions of the resources, as well as additional resources not included in this book, can be found online at https://beyondcourts.org/.

The resources in this book are produced as separate chapters and are organized to move readers from learning to action. "Criminal Courts 101" (Chapter One) walks readers through the path of a typical criminal court case, from arrest to sentencing, exposing the violence embedded in every step of the process. "Common Questions about Criminal Court Reform" (Chapter Two) describes and critiques the most common reforms proposed to make criminal court more "fair," but which in reality only pour more money, power, legitimacy into the courts, and extend the reach of the criminal punishment system. "Problem Creating Courts" (Chapter Three) provides a more in-depth explanation of how diversion programs and specialty courts are examples of reforms that expand social control and entrench the system.

So what can we do instead? How can we collectively fight back and build the power to dismantle criminal courts for good? "Community Interventions to Shift Power" (Chapter Four) describes grassroots, abolitionist interventions (like court watching, bail funds, jury nullification, and more) that ordinary people can use to shift power away from the system and towards criminalized people and communities. "Defunding Courts" (Chapter Five) invites readers to consider extending organizing and demands from defund police to defund courts and district attorney offices. "No Such Thing as 'Progressive Prosecutors'" (Chapter Six) details the ways in which so-called "progressive prosecutors" have enlarged the resources, size, scope, and legitimacy of their offices and the criminal punishment system. Immediately following, in "Abolitionist Principles & Campaign Strategies for Prosecutor Organizing" (Chapter Seven), we offer other abolitionist organizing strategies that can shrink the power of the system and move us closer to a world without prosecutors and prosecution. Finally, at the end of the book is a glossary that includes key terms mentioned throughout.

We invite you to use this book to learn about the violence of criminal courts, imagine other life-giving ways of being in relationship with others, and act to dismantle oppressive systems while creating something new.

About the Organizational Authors

Beyond Criminal Courts is a collaborative project created by three organizations dedicated to ending criminalization and incarceration: Community Justice Exchange, Interrupting Criminalization, and Critical Resistance.

Community Justice Exchange (https://www.communityjusticeexchange.org/) develops, shares and experiments with tactical interventions, strategic organizing practices, and innovative organizing tools to end all forms of criminalization, incarceration, surveillance, supervision, and detention. CJE provides support to community-based organizations across the country that are experimenting with bottom-up interventions that contest the current operation and function of the criminal legal and immigration detention systems. CJE produces tools and resources for organizers to creatively tackle multiple drivers of criminalization and incarceration.

Critical Resistance (https://criticalresistance.org/) seeks to build an international movement to end the prison industrial complex (PIC) by challenging the belief that caging and controlling people makes us safe. CR believes that basic necessities such as food, shelter, and freedom are what really make our communities secure. As such, CR's work is part of global struggles against inequality and powerlessness. The success of the movement requires that it reflect communities most affected by the PIC. Critical Resistance is a national grassroots organization with members across the United States while primarily organizing through local chapters.

Interrupting Criminalization (https://www.interruptingcriminalization.com/) is a movement resource hub offering information, cross-movement networks, learning, and practice for organizers, practitioners, and advocates on the cutting edge of efforts to build a world free of criminalization, policing, punishment, and violence. Led by veteran Black feminist abolitionist organizers Mariame Kaba and Andrea J. Ritchie, IC creates resources, develops containers, and weaves cross-movement networks, building capacity for and with organizers and advocates working to end the growing criminalization and incarceration of women, LGBTQ, trans, and gender non-conforming people of color.

Introduction

In the United States, policing, criminalization, and punishment operate as the default response to all forms of conflict, harm, and need. Criminal courts play a central role in this process, and create additional harms, separating families, caging people, depressing wages, inflicting long-lasting emotional distress, among other irreparable harms. As we work to defund police and prisons, we need to challenge all carceral institutions, including criminal courts, in order to dismantle the entire prison industrial complex.

To build a society with the conditions for us all to flourish, we must imagine ways to evaluate and adjudicate harm, violence, and abuse outside of systems of surveillance, policing, punishment, and exile.

Why focus on criminal courts?

The majority of criminal court cases start with surveillance, policing, and criminalization in service of **racial capitalism, cisheteropatriarchy, ableism,** and **border imperialism**. Criminalization is a primary tool in establishing and maintaining these relations of power, and criminal law has always targeted people, communities, and behaviors in service of this goal. Instead of preventing or interrupting violence, criminalization has furthered the structural violence endemic to racial capitalism. As abolitionist organizer and professor Ruth Wilson Gilmore says, "prisons are catchall solutions to social problems."

Every day, criminal courts separate families, confine people to cages, depress wages, and inflict long-lasting emotional distress. For this reason, organizers must not only work to defund police and prisons. We have to dismantle the entire **prison industrial complex**, which includes courts, pre-trial supervision, probation, parole and diversion programs. At the same time, we need to dream and create new ways to prevent and interrupt violence, investigate and adjudicate conflict and harm, and invite accountability and transformation.

This means abolitionist movements need to focus on the operation, power and resources of criminal courts. Many already are. In this book, we'll share what we know about criminal courts and why they can never deliver justice. Many procedural reforms promoted to eliminate discrimination and create more fairness in courts simply prop up a system that is designed to surveil, police, criminalize, and punish. Instead, we are more hopeful about campaigns to reduce funding, power and legitimacy, and ultimately dismantle criminal courts. Of course these are also inextricably linked to fights to divest from policing and punishment and invest in community safety.

As we build a society that creates the conditions for us all to flourish, we are imagining ways to evaluate and adjudicate harm, violence, and abuse outside of systems of surveillance, policing, punishment, and exile.

Criminal courts are just one part of the prison industrial complex.

Courts are situated in a vast web of public and private organizations, institutions, and individuals that accumulate power and profit from the expansion of systems of control and confinement. Like police and prisons, they consume millions of (mostly public) dollars a year that could be used to prevent, interrupt and heal from violence. To date, organizing and theorizing has primarily focused on other aspects of this web, specifically policing and imprisonment.[1] This project seeks to intervene explicitly at the site of criminal courts, in ways that are connected to fights to defund and abolish police, criminalization, jails, prisons, ICE detention centers, surveillance, family policing and more. Even as we focus on dismantling individual components, it is critical to keep the entire prison-industrial-complex in view.

Throughout this book, certain terms have been bolded in orange and in order to provide accessible definitions. A separate glossary is also available on page 103.

Racial Capitalism: As geographer and organizer Ruth Wilson Gilmore has said, "Capitalism requires inequality and racism enshrines it...All capitalism is racial from its beginning, which is to say the capitalism that we have inherited is constantly and reproducing itself and it will continue to depend on racial practice and racial hierarchy. No matter what."[2]

Capitalism requires a division of labor and power. There are those who own and profit from the factories, the land, the intellectual property and the companies, and there are those whose labor is exploited to produce value that keeps the economy going. One of the ways our society differentiates between these roles and preserves the power of the capital owning class is by justifying these differences as racial hierarchies. Groups of people are classified based on real or imagined attributes and their lives are devalued on account of these traits. Criminalization is a tool the state uses to manage those discarded by racial capitalism, and reinforces race and class based hierarchies by marking people with criminal records and depriving them of life chances.

Cisheteropatriarchy: The oppressive set of assumptions that maintains that the normal expression of sexuality is one of a married couple of two people, male and female, whose gender corresponds with their birth sex.

These views permeate dominant culture and are expressed in everyday discourse, the media, welfare systems, and areas of law, including criminal law. These assumptions are apparent in the moral panics and subsequent attempts to regulate and criminalize a range of sexual practices deemed deviant such as promiscuity, pornography, sex work, one-parent families, and extra-marital sex. It creates the conditions for the criminalization and oppression of queer and trans people specifically.

Ableism: Ableism is the oppression people and groups to face due to a perceived or lived disability.

Ableism can result in the denial of resources, agency and dignity based on one's abilities, whether mental, intellectual, emotional or physical. As the Anti-Violence Project explains, "Ableism depends on a binary, and benefits able-bodied people at the expense of disabled people. Like other forms of oppression, ableism operates on individual, institutional and cultural levels."[3] Ableism extends to oppression that a person or groups may face on account of the social expectation to be sane, rational, and not neurodivergent or psychiatrically disabled.[4] Ableism, as experienced and structured, is inseparable from racism and classism. As we show in "Criminal Court 101" (Chapter One), individuals endure ableist oppression throughout the criminal process. The law only recognizes a narrow band of disabilities as legitimate and worthy of accommodations, even those can be deeply inadequate and often harmful, leaving many criminalized disabled people abandoned or further controlled.

Border Imperialism: Instead of seeing the rush of migrants at borders in the United States and Europe as the source of the crisis, the term border imperialism directs our attention to the border itself as the source of the crisis.

Organizer and author Harsha Walia explains that border imperialism encapsulates four elements: "first, the mass displacement of impoverished and colonized communities resulting from asymmetrical relations of global power, and the simultaneous securitization of the border against those migrants whom capitalism and empire have displaced; second, the criminalization of migration with severe punishment and discipline of those deemed 'alien' or 'illegal'; third, the entrenchment of a racialized hierarchy of citizenship by arbitrating who legitimately constitutes the nation-state; and fourth, the state-mediated exploitation of migrant labor, akin to conditions of slavery and servitude, by capitalist interests."[5]

Prison Industrial Complex: As defined by Critical Resistance, "The prison industrial complex (PIC) is a term we use to describe the overlapping interests of government and industry that use surveillance, policing, and imprisonment as solutions to economic, social and political problems.

Through its reach and impact, the PIC helps and maintains the authority of people who get their power through racial, economic and other privileges. There are many ways this power is collected and maintained through the PIC, including creating mass media images that keep alive stereotypes of people of color, poor people, queer people, immigrants, youth, and other oppressed communities as criminal, delinquent, or deviant. This power is also maintained by earning huge profits for private companies that deal with prisons and police forces; helping earn political gains for "tough on crime" politicians; increasing the influence of prison guard and police unions; and eliminating social and political dissent by oppressed communities that make demands for self-determination and reorganization of power in the U.S."

1

Criminal Courts 101

Understanding the general contours of what happens in criminal court cases illuminates the violence embedded in every stage of the process and in each of the discretionary decisions made by criminal court actors.

Introduction

In this Chapter, we go through a typical path of a criminal court case—from arrest to first appearance, grand jury and/or preliminary hearing, court appearances, plea bargain, trial, and sentencing. Not every case goes through all of these steps (and they may have slightly different names depending on where you are), but understanding the general contours of what happens in criminal court cases illuminates the violence embedded in every stage of the process and in each of the discretionary decisions made by criminal court actors.

Our intention with Criminal Courts 101 is to provide accurate but also generalized information about what happens during the path of a case—but things are different in every state and city. If you want to know more about how things actually play out in your local court room, you will need to do more research.

This print version of Criminal Courts 101 is a slightly abbreviated version of the complete resource which can be found online at beyond-courts.org/en/story.

Background on Criminal Courts

In the United States, **criminal law** and **criminal procedure** first emerged in the context of **settler colonialism**, chattel slavery, and racial capitalism. It might seem strange to illustrate criminal court like a machine. Criminal court is often glorified as a kind of hallowed and just institution, as if governed by laws untouched by human imperfection. We want to show it for what it is: a dark and grimy place where prosecutors, judges, court officers and police officers work hard, every day, to criminalize and control other people, most acutely Black, Indigenous, disabled, migrant, poor, trans, and queer people.

In the United States, criminal law, criminal procedure and criminal courts are intertwined with the dispossession of Indigenous communities and the captivity of Black people into unfree labor. To this day, criminal law remains a critical tool for managing the crisis that is racial capitalism. As we go through each step in the path of the case, notice the layers of oppression built into the laws, rules, processes, and procedures we're often told are objective, neutral, and fair.

When we use the term criminal court, we don't just mean the court building, but also include the legal institutions, processes, procedures, and actors that are involved in the progression of criminal cases. In criminal cases, it is the government—not the person who says they were harmed

---

Criminal Law: Criminal laws define what is a crime: the actions, activities, behaviors or statuses that the state condemns and can punish by limiting a person's freedom or by monetary sanctions, like fines and fees.

Sometimes lower-level offenses*, like "disorderly conduct" or drinking in public spaces, are characterized as violations rather than crimes because they don't give someone a criminal record. What ends up being considered a crime is the outcome of specific decisions made by legislators about what kinds of conduct

to punish, by whom, and how. Those decisions have historically tended to criminalize poor, Black, Indigenous, Latinx, LGBTQ, disabled, migrant, and radical left communities and persons.

*A note on the term "lower-level offenses." Colloquially we use this term to refer to charges that societally we think of as being "less serious" or "less violent," we also use this term to refer to charges which we think of as carrying a less severe punishment. It's important to note that those connections are often assumed because of the language used

and they do not always mean this legally. Many charges we think of as being "lower-level" carry potentially lengthy prison sentences.

Criminal Procedure: Criminal procedure are the rules of criminal court.

The rules as written tell criminal court actors (judges, prosecutors, probation officers, clerks, and defense attorneys) what they have to do in order for a criminal case to move forward. The rules are written by legislators who have historically given most power to judges and prosecutors, who also have tremendous power to decide how to interpret those rules. Their way of enforcing the rules is just as important as the rules themselves. Criminal procedure tells us what kind of proof the prosecutor needs to provide to justify a charge. It spells out the deadlines prosecutors have to provide the proof. It also dictates the kind of information the defense is entitled to

—who is prosecuting individuals or institutions based on a possible violation of criminal law. If the prosecution is successful, the accused person is convicted and punished.

Criminal court involves both criminal law (what behaviors are defined as a "crime" and what are not) and criminal procedure (the rules of criminal court), and each state defines its own law and procedures.[1] That means that there are at least 52 distinct criminal legal systems in the United States (50 states and the District of Columbia, plus the federal criminal system). They are all supposed to follow the U.S. Constitution as interpreted by the Supreme Court. There are some differences across states, but here we've focused on the key general features that are shared across state-level systems in the United States. We won't go into the federal system, but many of the steps of the path of a case are the same.

When we describe the path a case takes through the criminal punishment system, we're mostly talking about how the rules of criminal procedure are applied.

Illusion: Many people think the rules of criminal procedure are designed to make the process fair: to help guarantee that each side gets their chance to make their case, and that the outcome is determined in a way that is objective.

Reality: At best, these rules give the appearance of fairness, but they don't deliver. The rules are rigged in favor of the prosecution and against the person accused of a crime. We'll point out exactly how this happens as we go through each step of the case.

Throughout each step of a case, we'll present other common expectations versus what really happens. For example, we're told that "justice" lies in the

---

receive to prepare for trial or a plea and what kind of evidence can be produced at trial. Criminal procedure regulates the kinds of behavior, questions, and actions that are permitted or required when prosecuting, defending, or deciding a criminal case. Criminal procedure is the "how" of criminal law.

Settler Colonialism: Settler colonialism is a type of colonialism where the land and resources of an indigenous peoples are stolen by settlers who permanently form a society there.

The United States was founded as a settler colonial society committed to conquering territory, systematically excluding and eliminating native peoples and enslaving people of African descent for the benefit of White settlers. To this day, the U.S. state denies Indian sovereignty and reparations for slavery and colonization, while it celebrates and maintains the same legal political institutions responsible for dispossession and genocide.

center of the criminal system. But at its core, the criminal court system is not about settling disputes or truth-telling. It is not a benign pathway from arrest to incarceration. The process itself can inflict serious harm, including on people seeking justice for harm done to them, and it exacerbates racial, economic, ableist and gender oppression, control, and exploitation. What it successfully achieves is surveilling, disciplining, and punishing people, without producing safety.

Arrest

Police choose who, and who not, to stop and arrest. In other words, police make the law, they are not accountable to it.

Most often, police officers make the decision about who to arrest and for what. They do not make these decisions in a vacuum however, but instead as foot soldiers of an institution designed to maintain white supremacy and protect white property.

Illusion: The U.S. Constitution is supposed to protect people from arbitrary arrest. The 4th amendment dictates that the police can only arrest someone if they have "probable cause" to believe the person committed a crime. The police faithfully enforce the law and they cannot step outside the bounds of the law. When police officers make mistakes, the court system corrects those mistakes to make sure those never happen again.

Reality: To determine probable cause, courts ask whether a person of reasonable caution believes that a crime has been committed, supported by specific objective facts. The amount of evidence required for probable cause is intentionally not clearly defined. Here is an example: The police cannot arrest someone just because they don't like the way a person looks, but if, for example, they see someone running in an area the police say is a "high crime area" with a bulge in their pocket, the police could stop, and search that person—and that usually is enough probable cause for an arrest. Probable cause is a very easy standard to reach, and even if police do not meet that standard there are few consequences. It is rooted in "objectively reasonable" facts known to the officer at the time of arrest—and what is deemed "reasonable" is very much shaped by race, disability, gender, immigration status. Courts, judges, and prosecutors almost always just take the word of police officers, and rarely second guess them.

Generally, the police then work with the **prosecutor** to ensure charges are brought against the person the police arrested. Remember, it is the prosecutors, as a representative of the government, who press charges, pursue guilty verdicts, and punish, not the person who was harmed.

Illusion: Police departments and prosecuting offices are two separate agencies with a firewall between them. Prosecutors act as a check on police, make sure all charges brought against people are legal and fair, and serve the public interest.

Reality: Police officers and prosecutors work together throughout the entirety of a case. Police officers are investigators for prosecutors, they establish the basis for the prosecutors' charging decisions, and they serve as their key witnesses.

Key takeaways

☛ By choosing who, and who not, to stop and arrest, police make the law, they are not accountable to it. There are rarely any consequences in criminal courts or elsewhere for cops who don't follow the rules.

☛ Police and prosecutors work together and need each other for their jobs to matter. Prosecutors are not a check on police power, but an extension of it.

☛ The best way to reduce the number of arrests is to reduce the power of police to make arrests—by working to (1) defund,

---

Prosecutors: Prosecutors, often called District Attorneys or State's Attorneys, are lawyers for the government. They hold the power to decide who is charged with a crime, whether to prosecute someone at all, what charges to file, whether to request bail and how much, and whether to enter into a plea agreement. This is called "prosecutorial discretion."

In many places, the head District or State Attorney is an elected position, and this elected official then supervises a team of hired prosecutors (often called Assistant District Attorneys or ADAs) who actually handle most of the cases in criminal court. In a few states, like Connecticut, Alaska, and New Jersey, the head prosecutor is appointed, not elected. Prosecutors are one of the most powerful actors in criminal court.

divest from and abolish police, (2) decriminalize, and (3) make deep investments in meeting individual and community needs to prevent, interrupt and heal from violence and harm. Learn more at defundpolice.org.

Charging

Prosecutors have the power to decide whether to prosecute someone and what charges to prosecute them for. The charging decision is so important because it determines how severely someone will be punished at the end of the case.

Prosecutors look at the information the cops provide and decide whether to formally charge someone with a crime. This decision is when an arrest turns into a criminal case and sets in motion the criminal court proceeding. Prosecutors prosecute people on behalf of the government, not the person who was harmed (if there was one) and will continue prosecution even if the person who was harmed does not want to pursue charges.

Illusion: The prosecutor makes their charging decisions in an objective and careful manner, based on research and multiple sources. Their primary motivation is to protect the public interest.

Reality: Prosecutors make their charging decisions mostly based on what the police tell them, even though police officers often make trumped up or sometimes entirely false accusations. Prosecutors are motivated to rack up convictions to advance their careers, and almost always unquestioningly charge anybody who is arrested.

The charges chosen by the prosecutor matter because they each come with different possibilities for punishment. Punishment does not only come in the form of incarceration. A felony conviction—or even certain misdemeanor convictions, like "prostitution-related" offenses—also have severe implications for housing, benefits like food stamps, employment, risk of deportation, parental rights, and exercise of civil rights like voting and serving on a jury.

Prosecutors will charge any and all crimes that could conceivably be charged based on what a cop or witnesses describe. Often, many different

criminal laws can cover one particular behavior (for example, taking some-thing from a store). This gives the state a lot of power when deciding which charges to bring for the same behavior.

Convictions lend legitimacy (and drive more power and funding) to prosecuting offices. Piling on charges (known as "overcharging") also increases the chance of conviction; even if one or two of the charges are dismissed, there are still a number of other charges a person can be con-victed of.

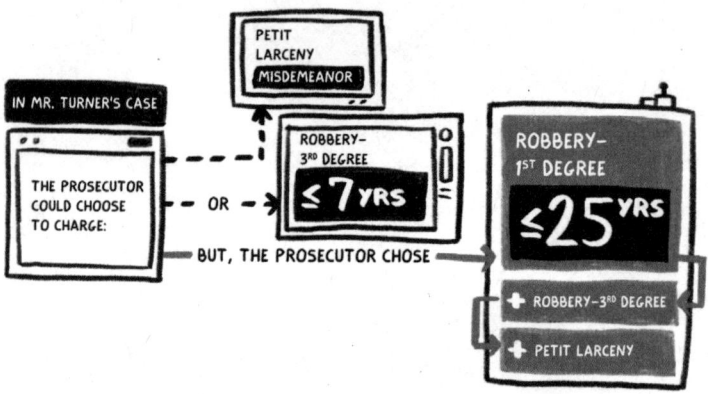

Illusion: If you are arrested and charged with a crime, you know exactly what you are being charged with and why.

Reality: When the prosecutor decides the charges, they list them on a piece of paper called the complaint (also known as the "accusatory instrument" or "charging instrument"). Although the complaint is supposed to put the person on notice of the accusations, in reality, it is usually a vague document that includes very minimal facts about the crime the person is accused of having committed.

Because prosecutors only have to lay out the minimum amount of informa-tion required to make an accusation, the person being prosecuted and their defense lawyer often know very little about what the prosecution claimed happened, what evidence they have and how they are likely to use it, and therefore how likely the person being prosecuted is to be convicted. Leaving the defense in the dark is a tactic prosecutors use as it gives the prosecution an advantage from the get go.

Key takeaways

☞ Prosecutors prosecute people on behalf of the government, not the person who was harmed (if there was one). This means that even if the person who was harmed doesn't want anyone charged or if they don't want to participate in the prosecution, the prosecution can still proceed.

☞ Prosecutors are entirely responsible for the charging decision. They have the power to decide whether to prosecute someone and what charges to prosecute them for. Much of their decision is based on reports from the police officers with whom they work closely.

☞ So much behavior in the United States is, and can be, criminalized, and the penalties are often very stiff. Average sentences in the United States are longer than in many other countries. Legislators in the U.S. have given prosecutors the tools to flex their power. Across the country, organizers have started campaigns to decriminalize offenses, such as sex work, drug possession, and poverty—that is, campaigns to stop things from being criminalized in order to reduce the power of prosecutors, police and the criminal punishment system to arrest, charge, and convict people.

☞ Structurally the criminal legal system is set up in a way that makes it more likely for a prosecutor to be able to secure a conviction if they overcharge and upcharge people. This is not just about prosecutors abusing their power, the system is designed for them to make those decisions.

☞ The best way to address prosecutor power is to work to reduce it, as well as the resources prosecutors' offices have, NOT investing greater legitimacy and funding into the office through campaigns to elect "progressive prosecutors"—check out Chapter Seven on reducing prosecutors' power and resources ("Abolitionist Principles and Campaign Strategies for Prosecutor Organizing") and Chapter Five on defunding courts and prosecutors ("Defunding Courts") for more information.

Arraignment

The arraignment is the first appearance before a judge. The judge decides whether there is a legal basis for the charges and, if the case is continuing, whether to jail or release (with or without conditions) the person being prosecuted during the pretrial period. The judge typically defers to the prosecutor for these decisions.

Arraignments are often very quick hearings, usually happening in five minutes or less, even though very important decisions are made.

Illusion: You get a lawyer just by asking for one and you have enough time to confer before any judge makes a decision.

Reality: Before any person accused of a crime sees the **judge** at their **arraignment**, they generally meet with their lawyer first. If the person facing charges cannot afford a private attorney, in most places they will be assigned a **public defender**, who are defense lawyers paid for by the government. This first meeting with a defense lawyer at the arraignment is typically very short: usually the defender will only be able to share the official charges and

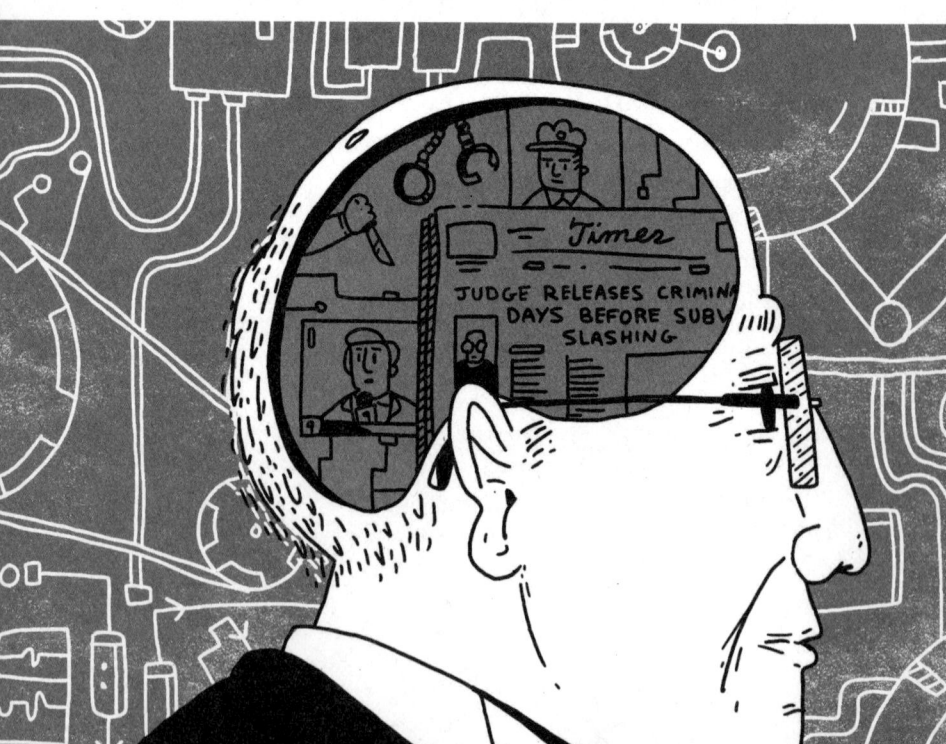

what the charges might mean for bail and potential **plea bargains**. In some states, the person accused will not be able to meet with a lawyer until after the arraignment.

There are two primary purposes to the arraignment:

☞ Official charges: The person arrested finds out what they are officially being charged with by the government (i.e. the prosecutor).

☞ Case ends or continues: The case either ends through a guilty plea or, much more rarely, through the prosecutor dismissing the charges. The other option is that the case continues and the judge decides whether the person arrested will be jailed or released while the case continues, and the conditions of release (also known as **bail**).

In some states, the stated legal purpose of bail (whether money bail or supervision requirements) is supposed to be about ensuring someone comes back to their court dates, in other states the stated legal purpose is to both ensure an accused person returns to court AND to protect "public safety."

Judge: The judge's role is to make decisions about requests or arguments about charges, bail, and pre-trial supervision made by the defense or prosecutor.

The judge is supposed to be impartial—not prefer one side over the other. But most judges are former prosecutors and their former experiences inevitably inform their rulings.[3] In other words, a judge often functions as a second prosecutor.

Arraignment: The arraignment is the first appearance before a judge, during which a person accused of a crime is notified of and answers the charges against them.

It is the beginning of the criminal case from the court's perspective. In some jurisdictions, a person accused of a crime will have more than one arraignment, once before the grand jury hears the case and once after the grand jury has voted on an indictment. Arraignments are short and impersonal appearances that rarely give the person accused a full picture of the charges against them.

Illusion: The U.S. Constitution requires that money bail be set at a "reasonable" amount. This means you should be able to afford your money bail.

Reality: Prosecutors request and judges set money bails at such high amounts that many people are unable to afford their bail and instead languish in jail for weeks, months, or years waiting for trial.

Money bail is not the only bail condition used, however. As awareness about the dangers of incarceration has grown, especially during the global COVID-19 pandemic, there has been an increase in judges ordering electronic shackling, home detention, or other supervision conditions during the pretrial period.[2]

Illusion: Supervision conditions are humane alternatives to incarceration, allowing the accused person to go home instead of being in jail.

Reality: These surveillance and supervision conditions are really just another form of incarceration and create their own kinds of harm and unfreedom.

For cases that continue at the arraignment stage, prosecutors and judges can decide to prosecute the case differently by funneling the case into a problem-solving court (sometimes referred to as a treatment court, specialty court, or status court) or into a **diversion** program. Whether a case is eligible for these different modes of prosecution depends on the charge, the jurisdiction, and the discretion of the prosecuting office and/or judge. While

---

Public Defenders: Public defenders are defense lawyers paid for by the state to represent accused people who cannot afford legal assistance.

Just because they are paid by the government doesn't mean they are on the government's side–lots of public defenders are very skilled and deeply committed to their clients' rights and freedoms. The quality of the representation and when you get a lawyer varies across jurisdictions and depends on the resources available. Not every state has an organization dedicated to representing low-income people accused of crimes.

In those states, attorneys are appointed on a case-by-case basis. And, even in places with dedicated public defender agencies, the agencies are notoriously underfunded and overworked, with annual caseloads spanning from 50-590 cases per public defender.[4]

Plea Bargain: A plea bargain is when the prosecutor allows the defense to plead guilty to a charge less than the maximum charge in exchange for giving up their right to trial. Over 90 percent of cases are resolved by plea bargains. Prosecutors have all the leverage in plea bargain negotiations.

these programs—whether mandated by prosecutors or judges—often seem like deals or bargains or alternatives to punishment, they actually expand surveillance and supervision, come with fees and other financial obligations, extend the state's control over people's lives for years, and can sometimes be a trap that ultimately leads to incarceration.

Bail: Bail is the process for securing release for someone who is charged with a crime while they await trial.

Conditions of bail or release may be imposed, such as an order to not contact someone, avoid a location, not get re-arrested, take weekly drug tests, or not leave the state. The condition that people are usually most familiar with is having to pay money—which is why many people use the term "bail" to specifically refer to money bail. Although the person is technically presumed innocent when bail is set, the courts have the authority to supervise and restrict the accused's freedom.

Diversion: Diversion refers to any formal procedural intervention, led or facilitated by state actors (police, DAs, or judges), that temporarily and conditionally redirects a person's path through the criminal process away from arrest, jail, charges, plea, or conviction in exchange for enrollment and participation in a program ("rehabilitation," "community service," "treatment," or "education," etc.).

Generally, diversion programs must create the possibility of closing a case without a conviction or with a reduced charge (like a misdemeanor instead of a felony). Diversion programs are similar to what courts call alternatives to incarceration or problem-solving courts, but often diversion programs come with the promise that the charges the prosecutor initially brought will be reduced or dropped.

Key Takeaways

☛ The bail decision is so important because whether someone is free, jailed, or under some form of supervision during the pretrial period can dramatically impact their ability to fight their case or their decision to take a guilty plea, not to mention their housing, employment, parental rights, and more.

☛ Supervision, whether in the form of home detention, a GPS ankle shackle, check-ins with a social worker, etc., and whether as a condition of release (i.e. bail) during the pretrial period or as a form of prosecution (i.e. diversion program), is really just another form of incarceration that expands the reach and scope of the criminal punishment system, and creates other kinds of harm and unfreedom.

☛ Arraignments and bail hearings are key moments in participatory defense campaigns—an organizing tactic that involves gathering community members to come to court to show the person charged and the court that the community does not support prosecution. See "Community Interventions to Shift Power" (Chapter Four) for more on participatory defense.

☛ You can fight back against the expansion of diversion programs and problem-creating courts and for the pro-health interventions that do keep people safe. Check out "Problem-Creating Courts" (Chapter Three) for more information and analysis.

Grand Jury / Preliminary Hearing

The next step after arraignment is a decision about whether there is enough evidence—**probable cause**—to move forward with the charges/prosecution. There is a very low bar to establishing probable cause so it is easy for a prosecutor to get the approval to continue with prosecution. First, let's tackle **grand juries**.

Illusion: The grand jury is supposed to create a limit on the prosecutor's power by making them prove to a jury that they have the legal basis for pursuing charges.

Reality: That is not how it functions in practice. In most places, the prosecutor decides everything about the grand jury. It is the prosecutor's show and their objective, generally, is to get an **indictment**.

They have control over (1) What charges to present; (2) What legal guidance to offer about how the grand jury should make its decision; (3) Which witnesses to present; and (4) Whether to go forward with the grand jury in the first place. Prosecutors want an indictment, and grand jurors usually agree. There is a reason we have the saying that most grand juries will indict a ham sandwich.

Illusion: Grand jurors have the power to keep prosecutors in check.

Reality: While grand jurors do technically have the power to refuse to indict and to ask questions of the witnesses, they often are not informed of this power (called **jury nullification**).

Additionally, it is actually a very radical and difficult move for a lay person, in the face of a judge, a prosecutor, court officers, other jurors, and general societal conditioning, to vote no and refuse to indict the person. Even asking probing questions can feel difficult and is often discouraged.

Probable Cause: To determine probable cause, courts ask whether a person of reasonable caution believes that a crime has been committed, supported by specific objective facts. There's not much more guidance than this general statement, but it is intended to be a low burden of proof.

The amount of evidence required for probable cause is not clearly defined. Here are some examples: The police cannot arrest someone just because they don't like the way a person looks, but if, for example, they see someone running in an area the police say is a "high crime area" with a bulge in their pocket, the police could stop, and search that person—and that usually is enough probable cause for an arrest. Before a grand jury, if a witness can describe a person engaging in a criminal act and they seem credible, that usually is enough for probable cause

for an indictment. The witness does not need to bring video surveillance, or medical records. A single witness is enough.

Grand Jury: The grand jury is a group of people selected from the public to decide together whether the prosecutor has probable cause to pursue charges against a defendant.

The purpose of grand juries is to secure an indictment. Although grand juries are seen as a check on the prosecutor's power, these tend to function like a rubber stamp.

Indictment: An indictment is a formal statement the prosecutor writes charging a person with an offense, substantiated through a grand jury or preliminary hearing determining there is probable cause. The evidence required for an indictment is low–all the prosecutor needs is probable cause.

Illusion: Grand juries are transparent hearings where both sides are able to present their side of the story.

Reality: Grand jury proceedings happen entirely in secret. No members of the public or media are allowed to attend. Not even the person accused of a crime nor their defense team can be present, except the person accused of the crime can be present to testify (and only during the time they are testifying). It is very rare for an accused person to testify since their lawyer cannot ask questions and you are not able to be present to hear what other witnesses say. The grand jury is a one-sided presentation by the prosecutor.

There are many paths to prosecution, and grand jury presentation and indictment is just one. Not all states use grand juries. Each of the 23 states that do use grand juries does so differently. Some states use it for felonies, others for a range of cases, including even misdemeanor cases.

Okay so what about **preliminary hearings**?

In some places, instead of grand juries, or in addition to the grand jury, there are preliminary hearings (sometimes called probable cause hearings) that both the defense and prosecution attend. The purpose is similar to the

---

Jury Nullification: Jury nullification is when jurors (whether as part of a grand jury or trial jury) vote against an indictment or return a 'Not Guilty' verdict even if they believe the accused person has broken the law. Jurors are traditionally not taught about their power to nullify.

Preliminary Hearing: The purpose of the preliminary hearing is for a judge or magistrate to decide whether the prosecution has probable cause to pursue the charges against the accused. They are sometimes called probable cause hearings.

Judges are often reluctant to dismiss charges at this stage, and it does not happen frequently.

grand jury: to decide whether the prosecutor has enough proof to charge a person with a crime. However, instead of a jury, that decision is up to a judge or magistrate. During a preliminary hearing, the prosecution will bring witnesses, usually police officers, and the defense can ask questions.

Illusion: Preliminary hearings are more fair because the defense team can actually attend and participate. The defense can try more explicitly to get the charges dismissed, whereas in the grand jury it's a black box—they have no idea what is going on.

Reality: In both grand juries and preliminary hearings, police officers are the star witnesses, and are treated as much more credible than anybody else. The defense may be leery of presenting their full case at the preliminary hearing because there are so many unknowns at this early stage, and don't want to risk showing their hand to the prosecutor, giving them an advantage.

Key Takeaways

- Probable cause is a very low burden of proof and so it is very easy for a prosecutor to get an indictment and continue with prosecution.
- The grand jury functions as a rubber stamp, not as a check on the prosecutor's power.
- Jurors do have the power to refuse to indict regardless of the evidence presented, although they are often not informed of this power and it can be difficult in practice to execute.
- We can definitely fight to open up or eliminate grand juries—and to teach grand jurors about jury nullification. Check out the toolkit at beyondcourts.org/act/jury-nullification-toolkit.

Court Appearances

Court appearances can stretch on for months or years before a trial happens, if it ever happens at all. During this time the defense will make legal requests for the prosecution to turn over evidence, but there are not strong mechanisms to ensure they do so. If a judge or grand jury finds probable cause to continue prosecution, the next step is regular court appearances until the case goes to trial, is dismissed, or resolved through a plea bargain.

These court appearances serve a range of different purposes: lawyers file **motions** and the prosecutor and defense update the court about their investigations and their preparations for trial or plea negotiations. These court appearances are supposed to help each side prepare for trial and for the judge to decide what evidence can be introduced at trial.

Illusion: If probable cause is found to continue prosecution, while there may be a few court appearances in between, a trial will begin almost immediately, like on *Law and Order.*

Reality: This time period for court appearances can actually be lengthy, depending on the case. In some cases, court appearances can stretch on for years before a trial even starts, if it ever happens at all. Court congestion (many people being prosecuted at the same time) can prevent cases from being resolved. The high stakes of the cases means that the defense may want to delay a prison sentence, especially if the accused person is free pretrial. A judge or court administrator can also delay a case by claiming that the courts are too busy to hold a trial, or that a co-defendant's case must be tried first. Sometimes the time period can be lengthy

---

Motions: Motions are legal requests the parties make. In criminal court, the motions filed during court appearances usually concern what evidence the prosecution will be permitted to present at trial. The defense will move to suppress (keep out) certain kinds of evidence the prosecutor may try to introduce, or to prevent the prosecution from using evidence of the defendant's prior convictions. The defense rarely wins on these motions. The defense can also file a motion to ask the judge to dismiss the charges, but that rarely happens. The judge can dismiss the charges if they disagree with the grand jury that there is enough evidence to sustain the charges. The defense can also file a motion to ask the judge to reduce the bail and to order that the prosecution turn over evidence. The judge has decision-making power over motions and the ruling on these motions will determine how a trial will go.

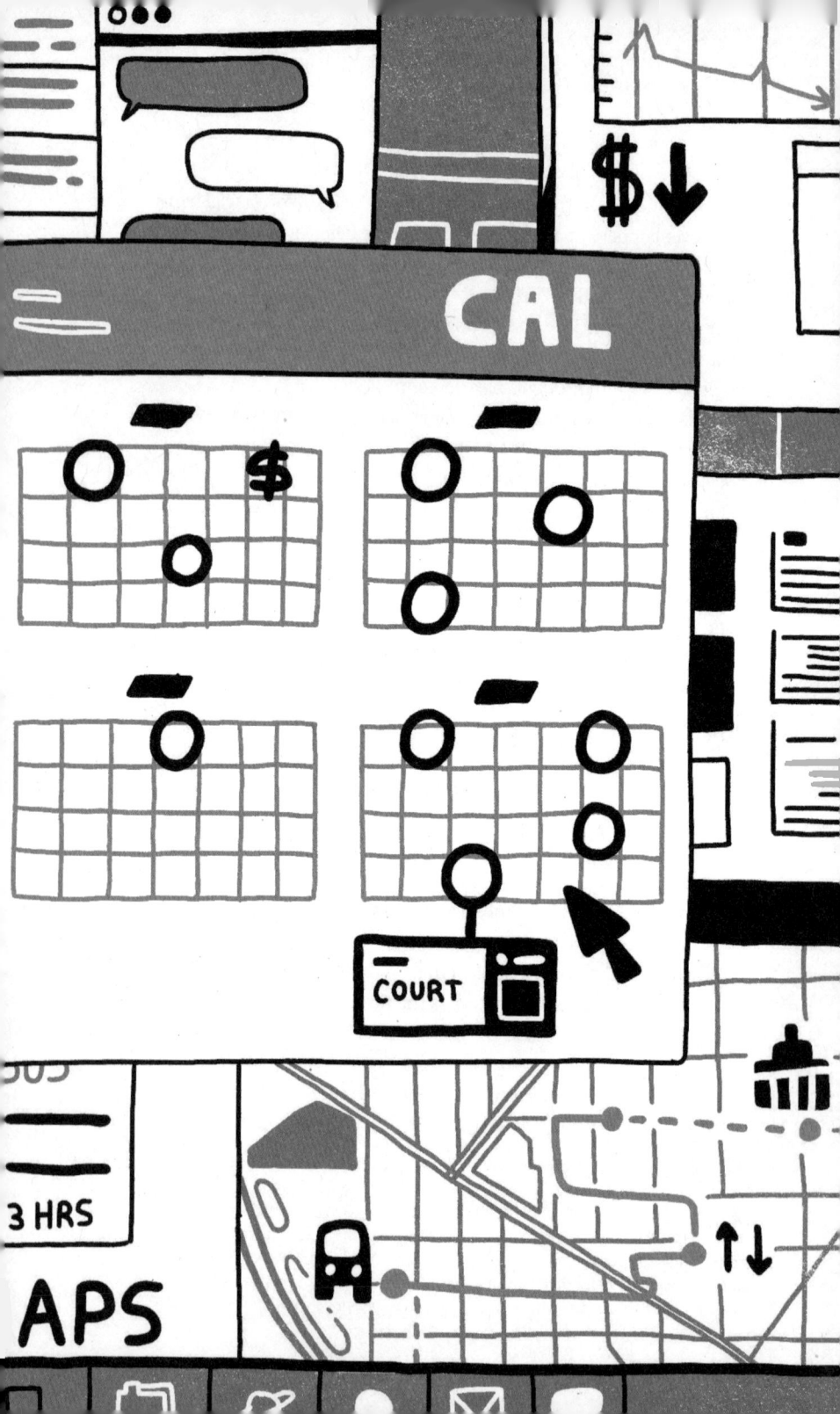

because the case is complex: each side may have witnesses and experts to prepare. Other times, the reason there are many court appearances is because the prosecutor's witnesses do not want to cooperate, but the prosecutor does not want to admit defeat.

The accused pays the penalty for the delays, either as time spent incarcerated pretrial or time spent coming back and forth to court for court appearances, unable to get on with the rest of their life.

Illusion: The defense has access to all the evidence the prosecutor has gathered before the trial begins.

Reality: Unfortunately, no. Although there are rules that require the prosecutor to turn over evidence, only they know what evidence they have. The defense attorney doesn't get to go through the prosecutor's files, and neither can the judge. It is the prosecutor who decides what evidence to give the defense.

Key takeaways

☞ During the lengthy period of court appearances, regardless of why they are stretching on so long or who is to blame for the delay, the accused person (whether they are in jail, on supervision, or technically free) remains in limbo, in the clutches of the court system, unable to continue on with their life.

- There are no strong mechanisms to force prosecutors to turn evidence they are obligated to provide over to the defense, meaning that the prosecutor often knows a lot more going into trial, leaving people accused of crimes to make decisions about their case—specifically whether to take a guilty plea or go to trial—while in the dark.

- Court appearances are key moments in participatory defense campaigns—an organizing tactic that involves gathering community members to come to court to show the person charged and the court that the community does not support prosecution. See "Community Interventions to Shift Power" (Chapter Four) for more on participatory defense.

Plea Negotiations & Bargain

The system is designed to give the prosecution all the power in the plea negotiations, ensuring that over 90 percent of cases are resolved through plea bargains.

As a quick recap, a plea bargain is when the prosecutor allows someone to plead to a charge with a lower punishment than the maximum charge. When someone takes a guilty plea, it is instead of trial and they can no longer go to trial in their case. Only prosecutors can offer a plea bargain, and judges have the power to refuse to accept them. Both judges and prosecutors also have the power to dismiss a charge.

Illusion: Plea bargains are agreements that satisfy the needs of both sides and a plea is something the defense elects to do for their own convenience, or because they are guilty. Indeed, when the person accused pleads guilty they have to tell the judge that they are pleading freely, voluntarily and knowingly. The judge will often ask, "Is there anyone forcing you to plead guilty?" The person accused will have to say "NO," if they want the judge to accept the plea.

Reality: Although an accused person has to agree to plead guilty, there are strong pressures to take a plea instead of going to trial, especially

if you are incarcerated pretrial and a plea could mean you'd be released sooner.

Illusion: Only people who are guilty decide to accept a plea bargain.

Reality: Because so much behavior is criminalized, it is true that a lot of (maybe even most) people who accept plea bargains have violated at least some criminal law. However, why people accept guilty pleas has less to do with actual guilt or innocence, and more to do with the risk of taking the case to trial and losing.

When someone goes to trial, they are tried for the maximum charges the prosecutor selects. If they lose at trial, in most states, it is up to the judge to make the ultimate decision on the sentence. In general, judges impose harsher sentences if a person takes their case to trial than if the person takes a plea. This is called the **trial penalty**. To avoid the trial penalty and the potentially lengthy sentence at trial, many accused people settle for the plea offer the prosecutor makes.

Illusion: The prosecution and defense have the same amount of power in plea negotiations.

Reality: Plea negotiations happen between the prosecutor and the defense and they happen outside of court, and outside of the view of the

---

Trial Penalty: The trial penalty refers to the substantial difference between the sentence offered by the prosecutor as part of a plea deal versus the potential sentence imposed if the accused person takes their case to trial. The trial penalty discourages persons accused from going to trial, despite their right to do so, constitutionally.

judge. It's like a private conversation, but each side does not have the same power. In fact, the power differential between the prosecution and defense in plea negotiations cannot be overstated—the prosecutor is quite literally backed by the full force of the state.

Illusion: Prosecutors have to abide by certain rules and respect the defendant's constitutional rights in these negotiations.

Reality: There are virtually no rules or laws governing how prosecutors and defense attorneys conduct these negotiations. Although a prosecutor cannot legally say they are making decisions based on the race or gender of the person they are prosecuting, there is nothing stopping them from considering that privately.

Key takeaways

☞ The system is designed to give the prosecution all the power in the plea negotiations, ensuring that over 90 percent of cases are resolved through plea bargains.

☞ People do not risk taking their case to trial because the system is stacked against them so violently that to risk doing so could mean a much longer time in prison.

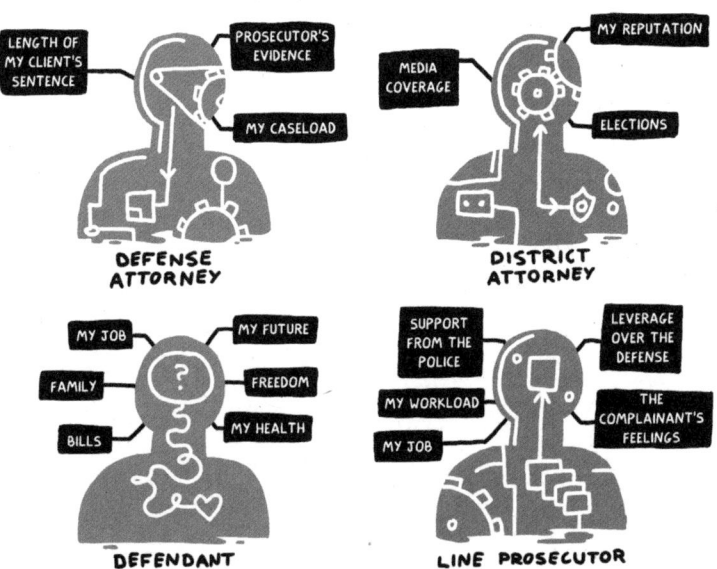

Trial

Although trials are prevalent in the media and popular imagination, they do not occur in over 90 percent of cases.

A trial occurs when an accused person does not plead guilty, either because they turn down the plea offer made by the prosecutor, or because the prosecutor simply does not make a plea offer at all.

Illusion: Trials are frequent occurrences. Everyone has a right to trial which means that accused people must get their day in court.

Reality: Although trials are prevalent in the popular imagination, they do not occur in over 90 percent of cases.

Illusion: Trials are the moment for the person accused to finally tell their truth, and vindicate their side of the story.

Reality: Trials are very scary for the person accused. Judges make decisions about what questions can be asked of the witnesses, including the person being prosecuted if they are testifying. Many judges allow prosecutors to ask about their prior criminal record if the person being prosecuted decides to testify in their trial. The potential trauma of being cross-examined by the prosecutor can be a deal breaker in itself. These factors create a strong disincentive for persons accused to tell their side of the story.

Illusion: The person who is being prosecuted and their defense lawyer only think about the trial when they get to that stage of the case.

Reality: The defense is accounting for what might happen in a trial from the moment the official charges are announced. Throughout the entire case, the way the person being prosecuted and their lawyer make decisions is about predicting how the trial will likely go, and often those predictions are not hopeful. A lawyer's advice to her client will hinge on what will happen at trial. The lawyer's assessment of how likely it is that they will win at trial shapes whether or not to take a plea, and what plea to take.

Illusion: The constitution entitles every person accused to a jury of their peers.

Reality: Prosecutors consistently prefer white middle-class or upper-class juries. And depending on the jurisdiction, prosecutors can easily orchestrate that composition.

Illusion: Jurors listen to each witness objectively and uniformly.

Reality: The prosecution's star witnesses are police officers, and in general most jurors (considering the kinds of people who are typically selected to be on juries) trust the police. Meanwhile, because poor communities and Black and brown communities are disproportionately criminalized, witnesses for the defense tend to be poor people of color.

Key takeaways

- The system is designed to ensure convictions through plea deals. It could not function if everyone who was charged with a crime took their case to trial.

- Less than 10 percent of people accused of crimes exercise their constitutional right to trial because the risk of losing at trial is so great and the penalties for losing in trial, versus taking a plea bargain, can be so extreme.

- Jury composition can determine the outcome of a case and jurors selected to serve are more likely to be white, middle to upper class, and politically moderate to conservative.

☛ Trials are key moments in participatory defense campaigns—an organizing tactic that involves gathering community members to come to court to show the person charged and the court that the community does not support prosecution. See "Community Interventions to Shift Power" (Chapter Four) for more on participatory defense.

Sentencing

Judges have a lot of power in assigning punishment, and sentences are also dictated by structural factors embedded in state and federal criminal law and procedure.

After an accused person has taken a guilty plea or has been convicted at trial, the court holds a sentencing hearing where the judge hears from all parties (defense, prosecution, probation) and then decides the punishment.

Types of sentences include incarceration, fines, probation, **Alternatives to Incarceration** (ATI), restitution, community service, and, in some states, the death penalty.

Illusion: A judge gets to choose whatever sentence they want.

Reality: While the judge often has discretion, the crimes a person is found guilty of (or pleads guilty to) often require a minimum (and a maximum) sentence. For example, in New York, if you are convicted of robbery in the third degree, you can be sentenced to a minimum of 2-3 years in prison, or up to 7 years in prison. If you are convicted of robbery in the second degree, the minimum is 3.5 years and the maximum goes up to 15 years.

Alternatives to Incarceration (ATI): ATIs are when a person charged with or convicted of a crime is offered an alternative option instead of incarceration. Participants must successfully complete the ATI program mandates in order to avoid jail or prison and/or to receive reduced criminal sanctions.

Alternatives to incarceration include supervision programs (typically with some element of "treatment," counseling, therapy, or employment/education/housing services), probation, house arrest, location tracking, community service, and fines and restitution. In many cases, whether or not someone is eligible for an ATI is decided by the judge or prosecutor after someone has already been convicted or pled guilty. Although ATIs have been widely embraced, these replace one form of supervision (prison), with another (therapeutic programs), but do not reduce the state's power to criminalize and intervene in people's lives.

There are also other laws that control aspects of sentencing (for example, authorizations for specific courts, three strikes and two strikes laws, primary caretakers laws, mandatory minimums) that limit the judge's and prosecutor's discretion.

Key takeaways

- ☞   Judges have a lot of power in assigning punishment, and sentences are also dictated by structural factors embedded in state and federal criminal law and procedure.

☞ Sentencing is a key moment in participatory defense campaigns—an organizing tactic that involves gathering community members to come to court to show the person charged and the court that the community does not support prosecution. See "Community Interventions to Shift Power" (Chapter Four) for more on participatory defense.

Conclusion

Thanks for walking through the path of a case with us. By now we hope it has become more clear that criminal courts serve not only as the pathway from arrest to incarceration, but they are also sites of their own forms of racial, economic, ableist, and gender oppression, control, and exploitation. While courts exist, they remain sites of contestation. Organizers, community members, people being prosecuted and their loved ones have found ways to intervene at different steps of the case to shift power from the system to the people and communities being prosecuted. Court watching, bail funds, cop watching, and defense campaigns are just a few examples. You can learn more in Chapter Four, "Community Interventions to Shift Power."

The processes, procedures, practices, and court actors that make up criminal court are all interconnected parts of a system that are rooted in and upheld by white supremacy and racial capitalism, and are designed to punish. Proposing tweaks to different parts of that system—whether procedural reforms or electing progressive prosecutors or judges—will not change what the system was designed to do. Those reforms might alleviate some harm, but the system will remain in place, fundamentally unjust and corrupt. If something cannot be fixed, then it must be abolished: what are the things we can do right now to shrink the size, scope, and resources of the criminal punishment system? What are other ways we can evaluate and adjudicate harm currently so we don't have to rely on the courts? What demands or changes get us closer to a future without courts and prisons and police and social control? Which ones build power and strengthen our abolitionist movements?

2

Common Questions about
Criminal Court Reform

This chapter includes a series of common questions well-meaning people have about criminal courts and reforms to make the courts more "fair" or "equitable." Like every resource featured in this book, we approach our answer to the questions with an abolitionist perspective.

We understand police and prisons can be violent institutions, but do we need to get rid of prosecutors and the courts, too? We are just not convinced abolition is feasible or wise and we have a few ideas on how criminal court processes and actors could be fixed or tweaked to ensure real justice for everyone.

Before we answer your specific questions, let get some context and history about the role that the legal punishment system has played in our society in the past and in the present day. We're taught that crimes are bad things that people do and that we need prosecutors and courts to make sure those bad people are held accountable, but it's much more complicated than that.

Criminal laws, procedures, and the courts have served as tools to organize society, and to designate some people and some practices as criminal, and therefore not worthy of care, attention, and dignity. We're taught that crime is equivalent to harm, but actually those categories are not the same. Not all crimes are harmful and not all harms are criminalized. People in power have changed categories of what counts as a "crime" over time, not to protect vulnerable people in society as they have claimed, but to advance their own power and property interests and to prevent Black, Indigenous, and other marginalized people and communities from building power and accessing wealth and resources. And when harm is treated as a crime, it exacerbates rather than solves the root causes of the harm.

As Andrea J. Ritchie and Beth E. Richie write, "Criminalization is the social and political process by which society determines which actions or behaviors–and by who–will be punished by the state. At the most basic level, it involves passage and enforcement of criminal laws. While framed as neutral, decisions about what kinds of conduct to punish, how, and how much are very much a choice, guided by existing structures of economic and social inequality based on race, gender, sexuality, disability, and poverty, among others...Criminalization extends beyond laws and policies to more symbolic–and more deeply entrenched–processes of creating categories of people deemed "criminals"...As a result, even as criminal laws change, the same populations continue to be targeted through ongoing practices...

The ways in which laws are enforced, policy changes are implemented, and policing takes place require our attention as much–or more–than the letter of the criminal law."[1]

So, when we talk about "fixing" the criminal punishment system, that assumes it isn't working the way it should. What we would like to suggest is that the system is not broken, but in fact is working exactly as it was designed.

Like policing, the criminal legal system (including criminal law, procedure, and the courts) has been a tool of **white supremacy**, colonial conquest, and capitalist exploitation since the first European settlers invaded the land now known as the United States of America. It is a system in which Black, Indigenous, poor, LGBTQ, migrant, disabled, and otherwise marginalized people have consistently experienced denial of rights by law and in practice.

Here are just *some* examples from history about how criminal law and courts have played a role in reproducing social hierarchies. These examples are just a few of many that show the fundamental purpose of the court system is not to protect us or keep us safe. Instead the history of criminal courts and criminal law shows how these institutions have worked to further the (short-term) interests of those in power at the expense of everyone else.

The criminal legal system has consistently been used to set up separate and unequal systems of justice, from the Courts of Indian Offenses that created crimes specific to Indigenous people (for example, banning Indigenous dancing, ceremonies, and cultural practices)[2], to the enforcement of slavery laws and Black codes which, among many injustices, denied Black people the right to testify on their own behalf or serve on juries.[3] After slavery was abolished, criminal courts enforced Jim Crow laws[4] by imposing criminal penalties on people who violated the laws of segregation and by railroading Black people into prison and convict leasing.[5] Courts in the South imposed the death penalty against Black people who were accused of transgressing the color line after show trials that all but guaranteed their execution.[6] Even today, a number of empirical studies show that prosecutors, judges and juries are more likely to sentence Black people to death than

---

White Supremacy: "White Supremacy describes a system of power that has its historical roots in the European effort for social, political, economic, and geographical dominance. This system of power is also key to how the U.S. has been organized to systematically benefit white people and act out of violence on people of color."[68]

white and Hispanic people.[7] As Angela Y. Davis writes, "In the aftermath of slavery, the death penalty was incorporated into the legal system with its overt racism gradually concealed."[8] Meanwhile, criminal courts have acquitted white supremacists who terrorized Black communities.[9]

Criminal courts enabled Indigenous land theft.[10] A 1823 Supreme Court ruling Johnson v. M'Intosh codified the "doctrine of discovery" into law, deciding that European settlers were the original "discoverers" of the land and thus had exclusive property rights.[11] The ongoing genocide of indigenous people was never seen as murder by colonial courts. Meanwhile white settlers used criminal law to assimilate native communities and to undermine their sovereignty. In the late 19th century, the Court of Indian Offenses criminalized Indigenous cultural practices, including dancing, healing and mourning rituals. Indigenous people were prosecuted for not working to the colonists' satisfaction.

In the 1920s, the Supreme Court issued a series of anti-labor decisions in response to the growing strength of unions.[12] Lower courts across the country regularly issued injunctions against striking, picketing, and other union activities. The courts also took no legal action against bosses hiring "private security" to brutalize (and sometimes kill) organizers. This legal repression, and lack of protection, contributed to the ultimate decline of organized labor's power and influence. It also illustrates the choice the courts made in advancing an anti-worker socio-economic and political order. Into the 1930s and beyond, government bodies at all levels used criminal and immigration laws (specifically the 1940 Smith Act,[13] the 1950 McCarran Act, and the 1952 McCarran-Walter Act[14]) to deport, surveil, and prosecute communists involved in labor organizing, charging them with sedition and treason.

The law and courts have also encoded the hetero-patriarchal domination of women, queer, trans and gender non conforming people, and they have exerted control over people's sexual and reproductive autonomy. Until the mid-twentieth century, in rape prosecutions involving an unmarried man charged with raping an unmarried woman, the man would be given the choice (usually with no input from the survivor) to avoid punishment if he decided to marry the person he raped.[15] For much of U.S. history, the rape of Black women wasn't even against the law. In the 1850s, an enslaved Black woman, Celia, killed her master after he raped her repeatedly over the course of many years.[16] The courts declared that because Celia was, under the law, property and not a person, she did not have the right to self-defense and was consequently sentenced to death by hanging. Criminal courts have also enforced bans on cross-dressing[17] and sodomy;[18] and over the past few years, several states have introduced bills,[19] and even successfully passed laws, to criminalize the provision of gender-affirming healthcare for trans youth. In the early 20th Century, states like Oklahoma passed the Habitual Criminal Sterilization Act, which allowed the government to sterilize a person convicted of a crime, because of the pervasive view that "criminality" was hereditary.[20] Although that law was struck down by the U.S. Supreme Court, states such as California currently still prohibit incarcerated people from having children and conduct forced sterilization on incarcerated people.[21] This legacy of criminalization continues with states prosecuting people for abortion[22] and sex work,[23] interfering with people's sexual and reproductive autonomy. In 2021, the Supreme Court allowed an anti-abortion law to go into effect in Texas, preventing people seeking abortions from getting the healthcare they need.[24] In 2022, the Supreme Court overturned Roe v. Wade and ended the constitutional right to abortion, resulting in the closing of many abortion clinics in states that banned the procedure.

Through U.S. history and today, police and prosecutors use vagrancy laws[25] to prosecute political dissidents, and people who are intoxicated, leftist, queer or trans[26] simply because they are visible in public space. These laws have been used aggressively against Black people generally, but especially Black women[27] just for existing in public spaces—for example a Black woman walking home from work at night could be arrested for soliciting sex work. Vagrancy laws do not criminalize conduct, but statuses, conditions, and ways of life. The laws give the courts the power to suppress and criminalize whatever behavior those in power do not like.

Whether through "broken windows policing" or just regular policing, poor people are arrested and prosecuted every day due to the criminalization of poverty and houselessness.[28] Despite widespread unemployment and a surging deadly pandemic, the Supreme Court ended the federal eviction moratorium,[29] leaving millions of families across the United States[30] vulnerable to becoming houseless or housing insecure. Things people have to do to survive while being poor are routinely criminalized and people who do not have permanent housing are more exposed to aggressive policing and prosecution. In addition, prosecutors request, and judges set, money bail at amounts people cannot afford so often that the majority of people jailed pretrial[31] are there because they cannot afford to pay for their freedom. Criminal courts across the country are not made accessible for people who do not speak English or for people who are deaf or disabled; many often fail to provide adequate language interpreters for people who do not speak English or communication access for deaf and disabled people,[32] barring their ability to participate in their own defense and leading to their increased risk of punishment.

It is well documented that racial disparities are embedded in every aspect of the criminal punishment system. Black people are more likely to be arrested, prosecuted, convicted and sentenced to lengthy prison sentences. In 2010, 8% of all adults in the United States had a felony conviction on their record, but among African-American men, the rate was one in three (33%).[33]

TL:DR—criminal law, procedure, and the courts are tools of social control that primarily harm Black, Indigenous, disabled, migrant, poor, trans, and queer people. They are fundamentally white supremacist, ableist, colonialist, and serve to uphold all forms of oppression. Criminal courts do not prevent or reduce violence, they create and exacerbate it. This is a central feature of criminal courts, not an aberration.

What if we made sure the court actors with power—like judges and prosecutors—were more diverse (in terms of race, gender, sexuality, etc)?

Over the last decade, increasing attention has been paid to the fact that the overwhelming majority (95%) of elected prosecutors are white, and 75% are white men.[34] In the federal judiciary, about 75% of judges are white.[35] It's true that the criminal punishment system has a diversity problem. However, no matter the identity, or even personal politics, of an individual judge or prosecutor, their systemic function and power remain the same.

The job of a prosecutor is to charge people with crimes, secure convictions on behalf of the state, and punish people, whether through prison, surveillance, financial penalties, and so on. The job of a judge is to enforce criminal law and criminal procedure. These laws and procedures are not neutral—they harm people accused of crimes, and compound their vulnerabilities and oppression. As we show above, criminal law has historically furthered the interests of white supremacy, colonial conquest, and capitalist exploitation. The rules of criminal procedure disadvantage poor people, people of color, and people who are disabled. Judges also hand out punishment at the end of a case. Prosecution and the judiciary are systemic and structural components of the criminal legal system—the characteristics of the individual people who inhabit these roles cannot change their structural function.

For example, we can look to the few places where Black women have been elected as head prosecutor. During the height of the COVID-19 pandemic, the prosecuting offices of both Kim Foxx in Chicago and Marilyn Mosby in Baltimore (both Black women) fought to keep people incarcerated pretrial in jails that were COVID-19 hotspots.[36] We can also look to the U.S. Vice-President Kamala Harris – despite being a Black and Indian woman and daughter of immigrants – as California's head prosecutor made a name for herself prosecuting Black women for truancy,[37] hiding evidence that would exonerate a Black man on death row, and denying relief to Black women who survive domestic violence by defending themselves, like criminalized survivor Liyah Birru.[38]

Abolitionist scholar Dylan Rodriguez warns us to think critically about any diversity effort undertaken within the criminal punishment system: "Diversity Equity Inclusion—their roots are in things that intend to secure and sustain the legitimacy of police power and other forms of oppressive power. [DEI] intends to build legitimacy around already existing institutions and their logics of power. They are not intended to transform those things."[39]

Okay, but what if we passed procedural reforms to make criminal courts fairer? For example, what if we passed stronger speedy trial and open discovery laws?

If procedural reforms were passed that ensured accused people had access to a trial without delay (**speedy trial** reform) or that the accused person had complete and immediate access to all of the prosecution's evidence against them (open and early discovery), this might lead to better case outcomes for some accused people. However, most accused people have done the thing they are accused of, so access to a speedy trial or evidence quickly doesn't lead to their exoneration or prevent their incarceration, it just ensures they are sentenced more swiftly, and in ways that seem more "fair."

Procedural reforms are both important—in places that genuinely do not have the relief sought, like jurisdictions that don't have speedy trial laws, or evidence laws, or right to a bail hearing within a timely fashion, or right to an attorney paid for by the state—and they also are a red herring. Because while they are important to have, they are also easily circumvented by prosecuting offices and judges, they necessitate new funding streams to the system in order to ensure they can be exercised, and they further entrench in our consciousness that it is possible to wring justice out of this system.

It is possible to organize for procedural reforms within an abolitionist framework.[40] We are not saying that you should not fight for procedural reforms, but as you evaluate where to invest your organizing energy, be aware of the traps of reformist reforms which entrench the power and legitimacy of the criminal punishment system.

Speedy Trial: Speedy trial is the constitutional right of people accused of crimes to be tried for the alleged crimes within a reasonable amount of time, without arbitrary or indefinite delays. But in many states, this right is rarely enforced with thousands languishing in jails waiting for their cases to be resolved.

What if there were more prosecutions of the real bad guys that typically get off easy, like police officers who hurt and kill people, white supremacists, tax evaders or people who commit white collar crime?

In our current criminal punishment system, there are already exceptional prosecutions of individual white supremacists, murderous cops, or billionaire robber barons—they serve as acceptable sacrifices of the system's own foot soldiers to maintain the status quo, as part of an attempt to quell unrest and solidify the legitimacy of the system.[41] The few prosecutions of the so-called "real bad guys" gives the impression that the system is addressing the underlying violence of policing, white supremacy, or capitalism, without actually doing so. It individualizes what are systemic problems.

We also know that when new laws are created to supposedly protect marginalized groups, they end up being primarily used to target them. For example, laws which criminalize tax evasion and financial offenses are more often leveraged against poor people than billionaires or corporations.[42] For example, the IRS audits low-income beneficiaries of the earned income tax credit at twice the rate as it audits corporations.[43] And "hate crime" laws are more often used against LGBTQ people and people of color than in their favor.[44] A 19-year-old woman in Utah was charged with a hate crime against a police officer for stomping on a "Back the Blue" sign. As the Utah ACLU chapter stated in an interview with NPR, "We consistently warn that [hate crime] enhancements are oftentimes used to single out unpopular groups or messages rather than provide protections for marginalized communities. This case has confirmed those warnings."[45] In August 2021, the Nassau County legislature in New York made police officers and other first responders a protected class under the county's Human Rights Law.[46]

In recent years when prosecutors have filed hate crime charges against people who committed horrific acts of white supremacist violence, like Dylan Roof and Robert Aaron Long, they have also asked for the death penalty.[47] Abolitionists refuse to combat violence with state violence because we know that relying on the death penalty, prosecution, or incarceration to address white supremacist violence, whether perpetuated by individuals or police, only legitimizes the criminal punishment system and further entrenches white supremacy. Additionally, arguing to send all the horribly, violent white supremacists to existing prisons and jails just means shifting the harm of that racist violence from Black and brown folks outside to Black and brown folks inside jails and prisons, where they have fewer options to protect themselves.

While rare exceptions exist, it is unlikely that we will ever see mass prosecutions of people in power for whom the system was created to protect. The criminal punishment system will not dismantle itself through prosecutions.

As Andrea Ritchie and Mariame Kaba remind us, "Focusing on arrests leaves the whole system intact."[48] Calling for justice in the form of prosecuting the "bad guys" only serves to legitimize and further entrench the system, further perpetuating the criminalization, prosecution, and incarceration of poor people and people of color. Abolition is fundamentally opposed to prosecution, and we must look outside the criminal punishment system for accountability and healing.

What if we transformed some criminal offenses into civil offenses so people were redirected to civil courts?

Civil laws cover everything from traffic violations to violations of financial regulations, and civil courts include traffic court, family court, bankruptcy courts and more. In a criminal case, the legal penalty can be limitations on a person's freedom (through incarceration or surveillance) and a criminal record. In a civil case, the potential legal penalty is usually in the form of monetary sanctions. When an offense is converted from a criminal offense to a civil offense it tends to mean that a person cannot be incarcerated or arrested, at least initially, for violating the law. Instead, the person will face a fine. However, turning criminal charges into civil violations is not the cure-all many romanticize it to be.

Even without the threat of incarceration, civil court can result in harsh and devastating punishments. Poor people generally experience worse outcomes in civil court. Financial penalties are a heavy burden for anyone, especially those who do not have disposable income and they can lead to overwhelming, unpayable debt. The failure to pay government-imposed fines is reflected on your credit score and can limit your freedom to rent, obtain employment, keep your children, and more. Responding to a civil violation still requires an individual to take time off work, school or other commitments to attend court, leading to lost income, employment and opportunity. Failing to appear for civil court dates can result in a criminal arrest warrant and potential incarceration. Additionally, you are not guaranteed a lawyer in civil court and must pay steep legal fees in order to be represented and have a chance at winning your case.

Often when civil violations are instituted as a replacement for criminal offenses, police officers still have the discretion to choose whether to issue civil summons or effect arrests for the same offenses. This is the case after the New York City Council passed the Criminal Justice Reform Act of 2016, which created civil violations for some of the top "low-level" offenses that resulted in criminal arrests (such as public consumption of alcohol, littering, and public urination).[49] When such discretion is retained by law enforcement, we know the results will be anti-Black and discriminatory. Indeed, data analyzed one year post-implementation of the legislation found that officers disproportionately continued to issue criminal summons to Black people.[50] As steps towards abolition, we must fight for full decriminalization, as well as to limit police discretion to make arrests.

It's important to remember that even under the guise of civil law, people can still be deprived of their liberty and experience punishment. From the 1930s through the 1950s, the U.S. institutionalized (i.e. jailed) more people in asylums, hospitals, and institutions than it would ever cage in prisons. Civil law gave the state the power to label a person with a disability as a "mental defective," "mentally retarded," "epileptic" or "psychopathic" and to then warehouse them in segregated facilities notorious for abuse. In 1946, the US institutionalized a rate of 700 people per 1000 (at the height of mass incarceration, the US imprisoned at a rate of 600 people per 1000).[51] Today, people with disabilities continue to face the risk of detention, institutionalization, and punishment under civil law. For example, under what is known as civil commitment, people with disabilities can be stripped of their legal rights, detained and forcibly medicated because they are deemed to be unfit to care for themselves and a risk to others. Civil commitment is sometimes indefinite and has even fewer protections than in criminal courts.[52] Just because something is civil does not mean it does not deprive someone of their freedom and autonomy.

Finally, some cases that start in civil court can end up in criminal court and leave people at risk of incarceration in jail or prison. For instance, if you violate a judge's order to pay a fine or stop doing something in a civil case, the judge can charge you with the crime of "contempt of court." Unless we end the possibility of incarceration or surveillance as an outcome (i.e. through abolishing the prison industrial complex more broadly), civil cases can still result in criminal charges, a criminal record, and the limitation of freedom.

Civil court is not a solution. In fact, the structural inequalities that shape our society will only remain entrenched and may even be bolstered by simply replacing criminal cases with civil cases. Instead of looking for a replacement, we must fight to eliminate criminal penalties entirely—i.e. complete decriminalization—and focus efforts on investing in the resources communities need to live well and be safe.

What if the legal system gave out more fines or monetary penalties instead of incarceration as punishment?

Removing the power to incarcerate is good, however monetary sanctions are not a just or equitable alternative. Fines (as well as fees and other court costs) only enrich the system we are working to dismantle.

Monetary penalties are already widely used in the criminal punishment system. Instead of raising taxes for the rich and politically influential, fees, fines, and court costs—which largely impact the poor and people of color who are hyper-policed and prosecuted—become a way to fund public infrastructure in cities and counties across the country. After the police murder of Michael Brown in Ferguson, Missouri in 2014, it became widely known that fees and court fines, extracted from the working poor, are a major source of revenue for local governments.[53]

And the reality is that most people who are saddled with monetary sanctions cannot afford it. This is why the total amount of national court debt in the United States is at least $27.6 billion.[54] The inability to pay fees and fines often results in incarceration and leaves people trapped in debt to the criminal punishment system. Despite being technically unconstitutional, debtors' prisons are alive and well in the US.[55]

As history has shown us, substituting jail or prison sentences with fines, for most people, will just result in incarceration, the heavy weight of debt, and furthering poverty and precarity.

What if we only used criminal court to deal with serious and violent harm, like rape or murder?

The cases being prosecuted in criminal courts across the country reflect patterns of policing, not harm that is happening in our communities.

Policing and prosecution do not protect public safety or survivors of violence. In fact, 70 percent of survivors of sexual, domestic, and gender-based violence choose to not call the police or pursue criminal charges at all.[56] Any reliance on criminal prosecutions leaves the majority of survivors behind. Of the cases that are reported, less than 1% are actually prosecuted, and even fewer result in convictions.[57] In fact, only about 6% of people who commit rape will ever serve a single day in jail,[58] and only around 0.7% of rapes end in a felony conviction. And these statistics were recorded after every state in the country expanded policing and prosecutions and

implemented laws and policies that were sold as ensuring a criminal punishment solution to gender-based violence (for example, mandatory arrest
laws, special units within prosecutors' offices for survivors of gender-based
violence). Given how well resourced carceral interventions are, these statistics reveal survivors' justifiable aversion to the criminal legal system for
protection or accountability, and the blatant failure of the system to deliver
on either.

When survivors of violence or bystanders do call the police for help,
the person accused of doing harm can be prosecuted whether the survivor
wants it or not. Remember, the prosecution prosecutes on behalf of the
state, not on behalf of the survivor. The court process is not in service of
the survivor and the survivors themselves are often re-traumatized through
having to relive the harm and by being forced or coerced by the state to
testify against their will. Once the case is in the hands of the prosecuting
office, survivors do not have any role in determining what accountability
or repair looks like beyond a conviction.

Additionally, many survivors of sexual, domestic, or gender-based
violence are themselves criminalized, prosecuted and incarcerated. This is
often because their survival strategies—whether being coerced into criminal activity by their abusers or acting in self defense to protect themselves or
their children—are criminalized. Mandatory arrest policies have increased
criminalization and arrests of survivors, particularly survivors of color and
LGBTQ survivors.[59] Nearly 60% of people in women's prison nationwide,
and as many as 94% of people in some women's prisons, have a history of
physical or sexual abuse before being incarcerated.[60] For those who survive
abuse, the criminal legal system, and specifically the court process, serve as
the next abuser through aggressive character assassinations, monitoring
their movement and phone calls, shackling, and invasive strip searches,
creating an environment of punishment and fear.

If we want to protect victims of domestic, sexual, and gender-based
violence, we can and must do so outside of the criminal punishment system.
We can start with providing immediate financial, housing, and healthcare
assistance, increasing funding to non-carceral, community-based domestic and gender-based violence service providers, and creating community-based options for safety and accountability that do not rely on the police
or punishment system.

What if we gave more resources to public defense lawyers and beefed up their offices to reduce caseloads?

It's true that public defenders are widely under-resourced and that this lack of funding affects the quality of the defense for the people they represent. As long as we have the current criminal punishment system, we should be funding public defense lawyers so they have the resources and capacity to vigorously defend people being prosecuted.

However, more funding for public defense lawyers will not change how the criminal legal system is systematically designed and constructed to disadvantage the defense. Even the most resourced, trained, and skilled defense lawyers are working in a system that is designed to convict and favors the prosecution at every step of the case.

A recent study shows that while holistic defense—representation that focuses not only on the criminal case but also on its collateral consequences—can shave off time in prison and jail for accused people, it had no impact on conviction rates.[61] Better representation has rarely proven sufficient to counteract prosecutors' work to punish.

Many people who are prosecuted feel like the court processes are opaque, hard to understand and hard to navigate. Shouldn't we try to make court processes easier to understand? Shouldn't we try to make courtrooms more transparent and accessible to the public? Similarly, many people feel like courtrooms are dingy, dark and scary places, shouldn't we try to make these more friendly places?

It is true that courts are often dingy, dark, and scary, and that adjudicative processes rely on opacity and inscrutability to entrench prosecutorial power. Anyone who has tried to advocate for themselves or a loved one in criminal court is familiar with the barriers excluding the public from courtroom processes. These include physical barriers that exclude people from entering courtrooms via police force; technological barriers such as restricted video feeds that limit access to proceedings; financial barriers such as fees to access records; linguistic barriers such as poor or nonexistent interpretation services; operational barriers that conceal decision-making algorithms like risk assessment tools in a black box; data barriers including the dispersal of public information in various, disorganized formats across a chaotic array of overlapping agencies; and more. Such barriers, by design, shield state actors from scrutiny and accountability. Overcoming them and thereby demystifying courtroom processes is a necessary first step for anyone challenging criminalization.

However, making courtroom processes more transparent, accessible, and easier to understand does not fundamentally alter the unjust distribution of power at the core of the system.[62] There are at least three reasons why abolitionist advocates should treat calls for transparency and accessibility with skepticism.

First, when advocates demand redress for injustices in the criminal punishment system (draconian sentencing, mass imposition of carceral debt, pervasive brutality), an easy first response from politicians is to agree on data efforts as a first step towards positive change: "we need a better picture of the problem, so let's invest in data." Lack of data, however, is almost never the real problem. Indeed, this kind of response shows an implicit disregard for the knowledge that people gain through actual experiences with the system, as opposed to top-down data collection.

Second, efforts to improve "data transparency" can actually expand and streamline systems of data criminalization (defined as digitized, automated surveillance used formally and extra-legally for purposes of social control).[63] In recent decades, a new regime of carceral power has emerged, with a huge quantitative increase in data aggregation by corporations and governments feeding into a qualitative shift in the mechanisms of criminal punishment, characterized paradigmatically by "risk assessment" tools.[64] The process of cleaning up, integrating, and digitizing court records to achieve "transparency" can accelerate these dangerous developments. In this way, calls for transparency may operate at cross purposes with abolitionist demands for less, not more, data collection—or, better yet, for outright data deletion!

Finally, it is worth asking: how friendly and accessible can courtrooms really become? At the end of the day, the purpose of these spaces is to restrict people's freedom, with judges and prosecutors relying on armed marshals to enforce the captivity of incarcerated defendants at the point of a gun. Advocates interested in reforming the spatial dynamics of criminal courts should look to non-reformist models such as Youth Justice Coalition's "Chuco's Justice Center,"[65] which re-purposed a juvenile court and holding facility into a community center and school.[66] That is to say, the only truly liberatory reform that can be applied to courtroom design is to turn courts (which often occupy central urban locations) into something else entirely, like schools, parks, museums, or community centers.

What if the prosecuting office prosecuted fewer cases? What if sentences were shorter? What if we reduced funding for the prosecuting office?

Now we're talking! These are reforms we can get behind. Each of these reforms shrink the size, scope, resources of the prison industrial complex. They will not transform the system in and of themselves, but they reduce the system's power and potential to harm without re-legitimizing or expanding the system's scope. We can build our movement's power, and chip away at the power of the criminal punishment system, through organizing for these intermediate steps on the road to abolition. Many abolitionists refer to these kinds of reforms as "non-reformist reforms" (or "abolitionist steps"), as long as they are also accompanied by a growth in power for prison industrial complex (PIC) abolitionist movements.[67]

If we do away with criminal court, how will we enforce the law? Won't there be chaos?

Just because we want to abolish criminal courts (and the entire prison industrial complex) does not mean that we want chaos or unfettered violence. We want to live in a world where less harm happens and in the instances when it does, people who have harmed are able to take accountability and endure consequences and people who are harmed are able to find healing. We believe this is impossible inside the current system and entirely possible outside the criminal punishment system—transformative and restorative justice practitioners across the world are already (and have been for centuries) experimenting with local, community-based interventions. Instead of purporting to address (while actually both causing and containing) social problems—such as poverty, homelessness, mental health crises, drug/substance use and addiction, and so on—with criminalization, our society could address these issues at their root and provide people and communities with the resources they need to live well and thrive—including, but not limited to, health care, housing, living wages, access to clean water and food, and more.

A central goal of PIC abolitionists is to reduce violence and harm, and we understand the criminal punishment system (including cops, courts, and cages) as primary purveyors of harm.

The behaviors defined as crimes—also known as criminal law—and its enforcement mechanisms—police and the courts—were created (and continue to be created) in the context of an unequal and violent society. Criminal law and its enforcement mechanisms were designed (and continue) to serve the interests of people with structural power along lines of race, wealth, gender, ability, and so on. Abolitionists are highly suspicious of both the law and its various enforcement mechanisms, which are not neutral and have been used as tools of intersectional forms of domination. Fundamentally, as abolitionists, we want people to pay attention to how calling something a crime serves as a way to order and control particular people in society.

For most of human history, we have lived without prisons, policing, criminal law, procedure, and the courts as they exist today. We believe we can build a future without them, too.

3

Problem-Creating Courts

Introduction

Diversion programs are often portrayed as deals, bargains, and alternatives to punishment that benefit the person charged with the crime. They are described as progressive reforms, as "off ramps" from the traditional legal system. Many diversion programs are operated in partnership with non-profits, hospitals, treatment centers, or community based organizations —their connection to community-based organizations can make them appear benign, if not positive.

However, offering treatment, counseling, or job training through the criminal punishment system is not the same as providing these resources directly in the community, outside of the court system. Access to care, housing, treatment and resources should never come at the cost of an arrest or prosecution. Rather than offer a community much-needed resources, diversion courts and programs create coercive, burdensome requirements that trap people further in cycles of criminalization and punishment. They do not meaningfully address the deep social problems (such as poverty, racism, houselessness, drug prohibition, an unsafe or unregulated drug supply, and so on) that make individuals vulnerable to criminalization. Instead of structural reform that fulfills our collective responsibility to meet individual and community needs, these diversion programs offload that responsibility onto criminalized people, their families, and communities, a process sociologist Reuban Miller calls carceral devolution.1

A note about "crime":

☛ Criminal laws, procedures, and the courts have served as tools to organize society, and to designate some people and some practices as criminal, and therefore not worthy of care, attention, and dignity. We're taught that crime is equivalent to harm, but actually those categories are not the same. Not all crimes are harmful and not all harms are criminalized.[2] People in power have changed categories of what counts as a "crime" over time, not to protect vulnerable people in society as they have claimed, but to advance their own power and property interests and to prevent Black, Indigenous, and other marginalized people and communities from building power and accessing wealth and resources. And when harm is treated as a crime, it exacerbates rather than solves the root causes of the harm.[3]

What do we mean by diversion?

Diversion refers to any formal procedural intervention, led or facilitated by state actors (specifically police, prosecutors, probation/pretrial services, or judges), that temporarily and conditionally redirects a person's path through the criminal process away from arrest, jail, charges, or conviction in exchange for participation and successful completion of some kind of program or requirements (such as "anger management" classes, mental health or drug "treatment," restorative justice circles, community service, or counseling). Diversion programs led by prosecutors and by judges (the latter referred to as specialty courts or "problem solving" courts) are two of the most common, and popular, kinds of diversion; in the United States alone, there are currently at least 121 prosecutor-led diversion programs[4] and over 4,000 specialty courts.[5] The major difference between the two is that prosecutor-led diversion programs are created, designed, monitored, and controlled by prosecutors, without the involvement of other court actors, including defense attorneys, whereas specialty courts (such as drug courts, mental health courts, veterans courts, trafficking courts, and so on) often require prosecutor approval over whose case can be "diverted" through the diversion court program, but otherwise are under the complete control of judges. This means that in both, the prosecutor or judge respectively has the power to decide the diversion program's eligibility criteria, to impose restrictions, to monitor progress, and to decide what constitutes the program participants' failures or successes. While defense attorneys are often consulted in the formation of these programs, their power is limited to advocating on behalf of their clients to be accepted into the program–in some places, a defense attorney cannot even prevent their client from being evaluated for the program even if they do not want to participate in it. Ultimately the judge and/or prosecutor make the decisions and set the terms. Depending on the jurisdiction, prosecutor-led diversion can be offered pre- or post-charging, as well as post-plea, while most (but not all) specialty courts are only offered post-plea.

Prosecutor-led diversion programs and specialty courts are just two examples of carceral devolution. It is not a coincidence that these diversion programs started proliferating in the United States in the late 1960s, as support for deinstitutionalization and decarceration grew, and as neoliberal policies,[6] described by Ruth Wilson Gilmore as "organized abandonment,"[7] proliferated. As Gilmore contends, mass incarceration and devolution are trends that go hand-in-hand.[8] Diversion programs and specialty courts allowed the state to say it was taking action to curb incarceration, while simultaneously transferring the responsibility of social welfare from the government onto private, for-profit companies, and nonprofit agencies. Diversion programs and specialty courts have only become more popular over the last two decades amidst both the wreckage of over 40 years of state and capital divestment, as well as a growing bipartisan consensus to "end mass incarceration."

As it becomes less popular to put people in cages (for moral, but also financial, reasons), the legal system is imposing new forms of social control under the guise of coerced treatment, care or services. As geographer Brett Story explains, carceral devolution "is how the carceral state is restructuring itself in the face of its legitimacy crisis."[9] Diversion programs are not in opposition to the carceral state; in fact, they are a part of the state's adaptive work to continuously legitimize itself, and are then used as a justification to increase funding to the legal system to fortify the system even more. Diversion programs can, and most often do, become a pathway to incarceration–imposing burdensome conditions of surveillance and control that people can't meet, and which are often punishable by incarceration.[10] The only kind of diversion these programs actually succeed at is diverting people's attention from the systemic problems they attempt to bandaid over.

To support abolitionist organizers fighting the creation, continuation, or expansion of prosecutor-led diversion programs and specialty courts–specifically in the name of reform–we have created data-supported talking points to push back on some of the most popular iterations of these programs: *drug courts, mental health courts, trafficking courts, and restorative justice diversion programs.* While all of these programs share some core features that we distill below, each has specificities that deserve close scrutiny. After discussing their similarities, we offer a compilation of news reporting, academic articles, peer reviewed studies, first hand testimonials, and takeaways on each specific program for you to use in your communities and organizing.

We have also compiled data-supported talking points for the investments that are proven to create health and safety: *supportive and affordable housing, healthy food, clean water and air, high quality education, guaranteed basic income, well-paying employment, affordable and accessible community-based healthcare, and community-based drug treatment and harm reduction services.* The solutions are not out of reach; we just need to fight for them and not accept reformist solutions that perpetuate and further criminalization and social control.

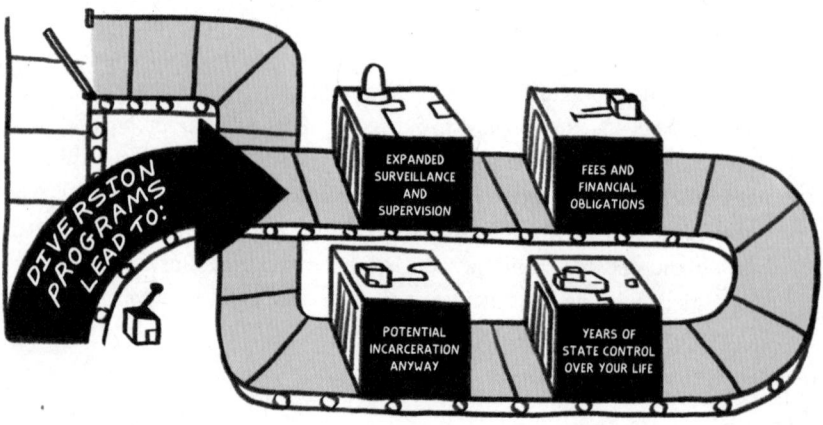

DIVERSION PROGRAMS LEAD TO:

EXPANDED SURVEILLANCE AND SUPERVISION

FEES AND FINANCIAL OBLIGATIONS

POTENTIAL INCARCERATION ANYWAY

YEARS OF STATE CONTROL OVER YOUR LIFE

Diversion is Social Control

For abolitionists, the fact that prosecutor-led diversion programs and specialty courts maintain and entrench the legitimacy of the carceral state is just one reason to oppose them. In addition, these programs: 1) extend the scope of the criminal punishment system into the community; 2) widen the net of people under carceral control; 3) increase the power, resources, and reach of prosecutors and judges (and the criminal punishment system more broadly); 4) further neoliberal logics of individual responsibility that uphold the criminal punishment system; and 5) are more concerned with control and submission than health and well-being. Diversion programs deprive people of self-determination through a logic of white paternalistic "care through control." Given the racial demographics of the people targeted by the carceral system, this kind of paternalism evokes the country's long tradition of racial subordination, dating back to chattel slavery.[11] Advocates of diversion programs have an explicit approach of white saviorism, framing the programs and their intervention into and control of people's lives as "help" that participants must be grateful for.

Diversion programs extend the scope of the criminal punishment system into the community.

In 1979, sociologist Stanley Cohen cautioned that the creation of so-called community alternatives would only further blur the boundaries between prison and community. Four decades ago, he wrote, "Programs reproduce rules (for example about security, curfew, permitted visitors, drugs) which are close to that of the institution itself. Indeed it becomes difficult to distinguish a very "open" prison (with liberal provision for work release, home release, outside education) from a very "closed" halfway house."[12]

Instead of being an off-ramp to prosecution and incarceration, diversion programs just punish people in a different setting, while retaining the same qualities of regular prosecution (controlling movement, regular check-ins, using incarceration as a constant threat). The people who administer the programs–whether doctors, social workers, or non-profit staff–must take on the coercive roles alongside police, guards, and probation officers. Diversion programs thereby conscript community actors into monitoring and policing people who are criminalized. The programs continue the functions of prosecution and the prison, while purporting to be a replacement. They extend the scope of the criminal punishment system into communities and onto community-based organizations and actors.

Diversion programs widen the net of people under carceral control.

Police always have the power to choose not to arrest someone and divert them from the system entirely–and often exercise that power for particular people and communities. Prosecutors have always had the option to choose to not prosecute a case and divert someone away from the system entirely. Judges have always had the option to dismiss people's cases through various legal vehicles. By contrast, formal diversion programs do not divert people *away* from the system but actually *further into* the system, by keeping people subject to the system's carceral control—just in a programmatic or "treatment"-based setting. Diversion programs also do not prevent the violence of policing, nor undermine the legitimacy of the police; indeed, diversion requires policing. In most specialty courts and prosecutor-led diversion programs, the only people who are eligible are people charged with what political scientist Marie Gottschalk calls non, non, nons ("non-serious, nonviolent, non-sex-related" offenses).[13] These charges include loitering, trespassing, drug possession, and other charges that many would agree should be outright dismissed or never brought in the first place or used to justify an arrest. Instead, formal diversion programs provide an avenue to keep people charged with these offenses in the clutches of the system, under the guise of treatment or re-habilitative programs, thereby widening the net of people under carceral control. And equally problematic, diversion programs legitimize the incarceration of the "undeserving." *They are an obstacle to what is really needed: complete decriminalization.*

Diversion programs increase the power, resources, and reach of the criminal punishment system.

As law professor Erin Collins has pointed out, **problem-solving courts** primarily serve to enlarge the power of judges and prosecutors and to expand the scope and control of the criminal punishment system, at the expense of their purported "treatment" goals.[14] The purpose of a court is to prosecute someone for participating in a criminalized activity; diversion programs and specialty courts shift that into something larger as they prosecute and criminalize people based on who they are or the circumstances of poverty, drug use, or mental health they find themselves in. This kind of court makes it socially acceptable, as a matter of principle, to treat people whose identity is criminalized (i.e. they use drugs, they are a veteran, they are houseless) as proper subjects for the court to control and manage. Through these programs, prosecutors and judges are given the authority to make decisions and deliver consequences for behaviors that are not necessarily illegal, all in the name of supposed recovery or rehabilitation.

It's important to note that, despite authorities' insistence otherwise, the traditional legal system imposes consequences for behaviors that are not explicitly illegal all the time. For example, there is nothing technically illegal or punishable about not having a job, but prosecutors may offer a better plea deal to someone who is employed rather than to someone who is unemployed. Or they will offer a reduced sentence to someone because they're in a treatment program while refusing to offer a reduced sentence to someone who isn't interested in enrolling in a treatment program. *But diversion courts often attempt to regulate people's behavior in more extreme ways than traditional courts, thus extending the scope of the state's criminalization apparatus.*

For example, diversion programs can and do impose consequences for someone being late to a therapy appointment or losing their job in a way that traditional courts (outside of imposing violations of conditions of probation or parole) may not. Diversion programs also give individuals without medical or healthcare expertise (i.e. prosecutors and judges) authority to engage in medical decision making.[15] The power creep of these diversion programs and specialty courts is extreme and ever-snowballing in this era of bipartisan carceral humanism.[16]

Problem-Solving Courts: Problem-solving courts are specialized criminal courts that offer enhanced supervision and "treatment" in addition to or in lieu of incarceration.

Oftentimes, the person being prosecuted needs to plead guilty to the top charge and then if they complete the program successfully, the conviction will be eligible for expungement (although this doesn't always occur in practice).[25] There are many kinds of problem- solving courts but they generally fall into three categories: **(1)** "treatment" courts, such as mental health courts and drug courts; **(2)** offense-specific courts, such as domestic violence courts and community courts; and **(3)** status courts, such as veterans courts and homelessness courts. As law professor, Erin Collins explains, "Despite this diversity, the universe of problem-solving courts is united by a common claim, namely, that these courts solve a problem that would otherwise lead to repeated interaction with the criminal legal system."[26] As with alternatives to incarceration, problem solving courts preserve the state's power to criminalize, but do it in new, and seemingly less offensive ways than incarceration.

The power creep extends to the increase in resources diverted to the criminal punishment system to administer these programs. Many prosecutors, and especially so-called "progressive prosecutors," request budget increases to start and run diversion programs.[17] Service providers and non-profits are contracted by the courts, prosecutors' office, or government to hire staff and run these programs. These programs provide further justification for enlarging the resources, and therefore the power, of the prison industrial complex.

Diversion programs further neoliberal logics of individual responsibility.

The logic that undergirds diversion programs (whether prosecutor-led or specialty courts) is one of individual responsibility.[18] A person who has been arrested is filtered into a diversion program because of conclusions made by prosecutors or judges about who they are or their alleged behavior (whether drug use, involvement in the sex trades, mental health, homelessness, status as a young person or veteran, etc.). The purported goal of the program is for the person to resolve these underlying "issues" through their participation in the program.

The focus is entirely on the person's character and behavior, not on the structural conditions, systems, institutions, or economies that organize their communities and lives, such as racism, patriarchy, poverty, organized state and capital abandonment or criminalization itself. This neoliberal logic of individual responsibility is the same logic that upholds the criminal punishment system: behaviors classified as crime are depicted as the result of bad decisions by deviant people who deserve to be punished, not as the result of chronic structural divestment and oppression. Ironically, this all also exposes how fundamentally these programs have an inconsistent logic: they are trying to impose "individual accountability" for behaviors that these programs admit may not have been willful, but instead are at least in part due to structural or broader social forces, such as poverty.

Diversion programs are more concerned with control and submission than health and well-being.

Finally, studies have shown[19] that judges and prosecutors reject interventions or treatment options that better address underlying criminalized health concerns if they also result in the diminishment of judicial power or control. As sociologist Rebecca Tiger has written, "Drug court advocates are motivated both by the desire to keep [people who use drugs] out of prison but also by the desire to keep them under the supervision of the courts and have argued, in journal articles and editorials, strenuously against criminal justice reforms that seek to minimize the criminal justice system's control over illicit drug users and/or permit people to access treatment without judicial monitoring and oversight."[20]

Fundamentally, these programs are rooted in mistrust and suspicion of people accused of crimes. These programs communicate that people who are accused of crimes cannot be trusted to take care of themselves if given the resources.[21] But there is little evidence to support this paternalistic and harmful claim. *We know that providing voluntary, free/affordable, and accessible resources and services (like housing, healthcare, harm reduction resources, drug treatment, counseling and mental health treatment) directly in the community are better for people's health and well-being.*[22] Again and again, the research confirms that individual and community health and wellbeing is best understood structurally.[23] This depends less on individual behavior and more on the social determinants of health, which require significant investment in public goods to guarantee nourishing food, clean water and air, affordable accessible housing, a basic income, and quality, accessible education, jobs, health care.

While these arguments may be convincing to abolitionists who are already working to lessen the size, scope, and power of the prison industrial complex, they may be less persuasive for people who are opposed to mass incarceration, but not necessarily to incarceration, policing, and supervision altogether. In the complete version of this resource, available online, we have compiled data-supported talking points to push back on different kinds of diversion programs and specialty courts, as well as to bolster arguments for the life-giving, health-creating investments directly in our communities. You can find the complete resource, including talking points, at https://beyondcourts.org/en/learn/problem-creating-courts.

As Stanley Cohen wrote in 1979, "The machine might in some respects be getting softer, but it is not getting smaller."[24] We hope this analysis, data, and talking points can support your organizing to destroy the machine entirely, and build a new world where everyone has what they need to be healthy, safe and to thrive.

4

Community Interventions
to Shift Power

While courts exist, they remain sites of contestation. At each step of a court case, there are ways to shift power away from the system and towards people and communities. Organizers, community members, people being prosecuted and their loved ones developed these interventions. They include: cop watching, court watching, bail outs and community bail funds, participatory defense campaigns and hubs, and jury nullification.

Introduction

Criminal court is intentionally designed to be a dis-empowering, individualizing, anti-democratic space. One person–usually a poor person of color–stands alone in court, separated from their loved ones and neighbors; meanwhile, the government fails to provide the communities that those people are a part of with the resources that they need to stay safe. In spite of this, every day the people most affected by criminalization and their allies participate in the system through bottom-up interventions that shift power and influence case outcomes. If you have ever participated in or witnessed community members filming the police, posting bail for a stranger, or packing courtrooms in support of the person being prosecuted, you've seen these interventions in action.

These kinds of organizing interventions are not PIC abolition in and of themselves, but they are abolitionist in that they provide opportunities to shift power, to build power, and to prevent or free people from incarceration or other forms of carceral control. As Mariame Kaba writes about participatory defense campaigns, "Some might suggest that it is a mistake to focus on freeing individuals when all prisons need to be dismantled. The problem with this argument is that it tends to render the people currently in prison as invisible, and thus disposable, while we are organizing towards an abolitionist future. In fact, organizing popular support for prisoner releases is necessary work for abolition. Opportunities to free people from prison through popular support, without throwing other prisoners under the bus, should be seized."[1]

Cop Watching

Copwatching is filming the police—or other law enforcement agents, such as ICE—as they interact with people in public. Copwatching can happen spontaneously by a passerby witnessing someone being harassed by the police. It can also be an organized effort–often called patrols–where people come together intentionally for the purpose of copwatching in a group.

The power of copwatching exists in the potential deterrence of police violence (whether the everyday or the spectacular) in the moment–cops often behave differently if they know they are being watched. Importantly, as law professor Jocelyn Simonson writes, "copwatchers' control over their own actions, data, and participation turns the tables on the traditional control that state officials possess to dictate the terms of public participation, and, by extension, to define the public to whom the system is accountable."[2] When you copwatch, especially with others, you shift power away from the police.

Examples:

☛ Since 2008, the Justice Committee in NYC has been conducting copwatching patrols, which they describe as "an act of self defense rooted in love and solidarity."[3]

☛ Berkeley Copwatch has been copwatching for thirty years, filming the police & serving as a hub for reports of police violence. Recently, they partnered with WITNESS to create a People's Database to gather and archive videos of police behavior.[4]

Court Watching

Court watching is when people from the public sit in courtrooms to observe what happens: bail hearings, arraignments, pleas, trials, and the everyday court appearances that constitute the delay and violence of criminal court. Sometimes this looks like formal monitoring programs, composed of volunteers or organizational staff who sit in courtrooms regularly to document what happens and report to the public the results of their observations. And sometimes this looks like family, friends, and supporters filling courtrooms (often called "packing the court") in support of a loved one who is being prosecuted.

Like copwatchers, court watchers serve as self-appointed watch dogs whose presence can influence the outcome of a specific person's court case. The prosecutor can no longer purport to be the only or primary representative of "the people." Court watchers also can share the observations they collect with the public to ensure accountability and raise awareness about the violence within the seemingly mundane and bureaucratic criminal court procedures, processes, and discretionary decisions of judges and prosecutors. When the observing, documenting, and reporting is connected to a larger social movement or organizing campaign, court watching can build power.

Examples:

☞ Some court watching projects, like Court Watch NYC[5] and the court watching initiative of the Coalition to End Money Bond in Chicago,[6] have used courtwatching to expose the carceral practices and decisions made by powerful court actors like prosecutors and judges.

☞ During the COVID-19 pandemic, Baltimore Courtwatch and other groups have been able to use virtual court watching as a part of long-term abolitionist organizing in collaboration with other local groups. Baltimore Courtwatch has tweeted the results of every single bail review hearing in Baltimore city circuit court since April 2020.[7]

Bail Outs and Community Bail Funds

Whether a one time mass bail out, or a revolving bail fund, this tactic involves the pooling of money to post bail and free individuals from pretrial incarceration. Most often the people donating funds and posting the bail are not connected to the person being bailed out, but are doing it out of communal interest in pretrial freedom.

When a prosecutor requests and/or a judge sets money bail, they do so purportedly in the name of the "community" or "public safety." In posting bail for strangers, bail funds refuse to let the prosecutors or judges speak for the community. Bail funds assert a different version of safety outside of the criminal punishment system.

Examples

☞ The Chicago Community Bond Fund,[8] which is part of the National Bail Fund Network[9]–a network of over 90 community-based pretrial and immigration bail and bonds funds, works to get people free through paying bail while also organizing statewide to end the pretrial detention system in Illinois. In 2021, as part of the Coalition to End Money Bond and Illinois Network for Pretrial Justice, their work led to the successful passage of legislation that, upon implementation, will end the use of money bond in Illinois.[10]

☛ As part of the annual National Bail Out collective's Black Mama's Bail Out[11] and connected to the campaign to close the jail in Atlanta,[12] in 2019 Southerners on New Ground (SONG) bailed out dozens of Black mothers and caregivers incarcerated in the city jail.[13]

Participatory Defense Hubs and Defense campaigns

Participatory defense hubs and defense campaigns are when people facing charges are joined by family members, friends, supporters, and advocates to deploy a variety of tactics to impact the outcome of individual cases and ultimately transform the power dynamics in the courtroom. These tactics can include creating mitigation packets or videos, conducting investigations, packing courtrooms with supporters, fundraising, raising awareness, pressuring decision makers, and attending to the needs of the person facing charges and their family.

Participatory defense hubs are often ongoing organizing formations that typically bring together the supporters of several different individuals facing charges whereas defense campaigns, although connected to larger social movements, are for individual cases.

Participatory defense hubs and defense campaigns show the prosecutor and the judge that the people facing charges are not doing so alone– their freedom from prosecution and incarceration is supported by a network of individuals, and often the larger public. In many cases, this has led to acquitals or more lenient sentences.

Examples

☛ The Nashville Participatory Defense Hub,[14] which is part of the National Participatory Defense Network[15] and coordinated by

Free Hearts,[16] holds weekly meetings with people fighting cases and their families. Participatory defense hubs often use the language of "time saved" versus "time served," in order to show how their collective organizing and support makes an impact in lessening the number of years someone might have spent in a cage. Since 2017, the Nashville hub has saved over 967 years of incarceration.

☞ The #FreeBresha Defense Campaign[17] shined international and national attention on the case of Bresha Meadow, a fourteen year old who shot her abusive father in self-defense. Utilizing actions like creating a petition to drop Bresha's charges, organizing mass letter-writing to the prosecution, raising money for legal fees, organizing rallies and vigils, organizing court support, uplifting Bresha's story and the story of other criminalized survivors on social media and mainstream media, and more, the defense campaign was successful in achieving a reduced sentence for Bresha and generating awareness about the criminalization of survival more broadly. The #FreeBresha campaign is one of many survivor defense campaigns connected with Survived and Punished.[18]

Jury Nullification

Juries have historically been the primary way that the community was allowed to participate in the punishment system. One of the most powerful ways to do that is to say no to a prosecution or a punishment while serving on a jury.

Jury nullification is the power that jurors have to find a person facing charges "not guilty," even if there is evidence to technically convict them of a crime. As a juror–whether on a grand jury or trial jury–you have the power to NOT indict or convict someone, for whatever reason, including if you think the law itself is unfair or unfairly applied.

It is difficult to find examples of organized efforts at jury nullification. This is because while it is perfectly legal for a juror to say "not guilty" for any reason, courts have decided they are not required to inform jurors of their right to nullify.[19] They can remove jurors for openly talking about nullifying. People have also been arrested[20] and prosecuted[21] for distributing pamphlets about jury nullification in front of courthouses. Additionally, it is a radical and difficult move for a lay person, in the face of a judge, a prosecutor, court officers, other jurors, and general societal conditioning, to vote no in the face of obvious evidence. Even asking probing questions can feel difficult and is often discouraged.

A juror who says "I am nullifying because I think the system is unfair" risks getting removed from the jury. Rather, a juror who wants to nullify will have to do so covertly. If they want to convince other jurors to do the same, they will have to build trust and educate other jurors. They might have to convince their peers to acquit on the basis of lack of evidence, even though they believe that the real reason to acquit is because they don't believe in prisons.

When jurors do decide to nullify, they are sending a message to prosecutors, police, and lawmakers that the status quo operations of the criminal punishment system are unacceptable. For abolitionists, this means that saying "not guilty" in one case can become a larger statement that the entire system is devoid of justice.

Examples:

☛   Paul Butler has argued that jurors in Washington, D.C. should (and have) found people not guilty of drug-related crimes out of a larger belief in the racial injustice of the system, and that jurors around the country may nullify cases with police abuse in solidarity with the Movement for Black Lives.[22]

☛   It can be hard to identify specific cases where a jury nullified, as jurors do not have to discuss their secret deliberations. In the UK in May 2021, a trial jury acquitted several activists with a climate justice organization, Extinction Rebellion, who were charged with causing almost $30,000 worth of damage to Shell's headquarters in London.[23] The accused activists admitted they had done the thing they were accused of, however the jury decided to nullify, presumably because they believed the actions of the activists were morally right.

Learn More:

o Jocelyn Simonson, "What is Community Justice?", N+1, July 19, 2017, https://www.nplusonemag.com/online-only/online-only/what-is-community-justice/.

o Justice Committee and Center for Urban Pedagogy, We're Watching: A Guide to Recording the Police & ICE, https://www.justicecommittee.org/cop-ice-watch.

o .Community Justice Exchange, So You Want To CourtWatch?, https://static1.squarespace.com/static/60db97fe88031352b-829d032/t/60dcd90f28a0bc210572cd52/1625086227389/CJE_Courtwatching_FINAL.pdf.

o Jocelyn Simonson, Democratizing Criminal Justice Through Contestation and Resistance, 111 Nw. U. L. Rev. 1609 (2017). https://scholarlycommons.law.northwestern.edu/nulr/vol111/iss6/12

o Raj Jayadev and Pilar Weiss, "Organizing Toward a New Vision of Community Justice," LPE Project, May 9, 2019,https://lpeproject.org/blog/organizing-towards-a-new-vision-of-community-justice/.

o Mariame Kaba, "Free Us All: Participatory defense campaigns as abolitionist organizing," The New Inquiry, May 8, 2017, https://thenewinquiry.com/free-us-all/.

o Survived and Punished, #SurvivedAndPunished: Survivor Defense as Abolitionist Practice Toolkit, https://survivedandpunished.org/defense-campaign-toolkit/.

o #FreeOusman Defense Team, Participatory Defense: Re-Defining Defense and Using People Power as a Tool for Liberation, https://drive.google.com/file/d/1Ing51KocILkxow-2qNa1oJYFotR2uQyk/view.

o Community Justice Exchange and Interrupting Criminalization, Voting "Not Guilty": A Toolkit on Jury Nullification, https://beyond-courts.org/en/act/voting-not-guilty-toolkit-jury-nullification.

5

Defunding Courts

Over the past two years[1] and the past two decades,[2] abolitionist organizers have waged campaigns[3] to divest from institutions that kill, harm, cage and control our communities, and invest in housing, health care, income support, employment, and community-based safety strategies that will produce genuine and sustainable safety for all.

And, abolitionists haven't stopped there. They have also extended defund demands to courts and prosecutors, who are also critical players in the prison industrial complex. Professor Brendan Roediger refers to courts as "an expressive component of police bureaucracy,"[4] while scholars Amanda Woog and Matthew Clair name courts as sites of state violence, coercion and control.[5] Like police, prosecutors and criminal courts are also promoted as essential to public safety. Yet much of what criminal courts decide bears no relationship to harms people experience. For example, in 2022, there were almost 13 million misdemeanor charges that forced thousands of people into the criminal justice system each year.[6] More than a quarter of all cases filed in criminal courts[7] are motor vehicle, drug and broken windows offenses,[8] so called "low-level" crimes that police and prosecutors pursued aggressively in cities particularly in the 1990s.

And when real harm occurs, criminal courts' default solution is prison or supervision. Those measures do little to prevent, interrupt, or heal harm, or transform the conditions that produce harm. Instead they make things worse. With little to show for themselves but social control, criminal courts play a toxic role in our society. Recognizing this reality, organizers are extending the call to #DefundPolice to a call to #DefundCourts by shrinking budgets for courts and prosecutors..

Prosecutors Fueled Mass Incarceration

At any given moment, the number of people accused of crimes and the number of criminal cases pending in a courthouse depend on the choices and actions of police and prosecutors, namely the number of arrests they make and the number of cases they file.

Professor John Pfaff has shown that increases in the number of prosecutors and case filings played a significant role in fueling growth in prison populations during the historic incarceration boom at the turn of the twentieth century.[9] As reported crime rates rose sharply between the 1970s and the 1990s, prosecutors' offices hired approximately 3,000 more prosecutors nationally, representing a 17 percent increase in staffing levels. As reported crime fell between 1990 and 2007 by 35 percent another 10,000 prosecutors were hired, swelling their ranks to 30,000. As the number of reported crimes decreased, so did arrests, but the number of prosecutors, and the resources at their disposal, remained the same. (Of course, crime statistics are notoriously unreliable, but politicians, police departments and prosecutors have used them selectively to increase their power and size).[10]

With increased capacity, prosecutors' offices charged more felonies per arrest. Pfaff shows that this increase in felony filings resulted in increased numbers of people sentenced to prison and fueled mass incarceration. Of course, it is not just prosecutors who are responsible for the astronomical number of people who are arrested, prosecuted, incarcerated, supervised and killed by the carceral state. Legislators, courts, police officers, judges in particular were and remain deeply complicit. The Supreme Court gave police departments more legal authority to stop, detain and arrest more people, with less evidence and with greater force.[11] It also shielded prosecutors from accountability.[12] Lower courts meanwhile routinely defer to police officers' testimony,[13] ignore lies and elevate them as experts.[14] Federal and state legislators, for their part, gave police departments bigger budgets to buy more lethal equipment and more officers.[15] And they also passed tough on crime laws that made it easier to arrest and incarcerate, for longer periods of time, which only enhanced the power of police, prosecutors and criminal courts.[16] Meanwhile, legislators and politicians refused to adequately fund their constituents' needs for welfare,[17] public health,[18] childcare,[19] schools,[20] and housing.[21]

But, as we show in Criminal Court 101, prosecutors are a powerful actor in the machinery of oppression. Prosecutors also make for good targets. And while there has been great attention and energy invested in electing so-called "progressive prosecutors," a strategy which we critique here, if we want to reduce the harms of criminalization and incarceration and increase the resources available to prevent, interrupt and heal from harm, we can start by reducing the number of prosecutors and their budgets.

#DefundCopsCourtsandCages

As we discuss here, many of the common reforms aimed at criminal courts preserve or expand criminalization, whether intentionally or inadvertently. And unsurprisingly, the country continues to arrest, supervise and incarcerate millions of people. Rather than trying to make criminal courts more fair, more transparent, more attentive to trauma, we argue it's high time to move beyond criminal courts. By doing so, our hope is to avoid the pitfalls of cooptation and to advance strategies that address the root of the problem: criminalization itself. We uplift the work of organizers who are trying to shrink criminal courts' power by cutting their budgets. Their work to defund courts builds on their ongoing campaigns to defund police.

The Black Nashville Assembly's campaign to "Defund Cops, Courts & Cages" is one example of such an approach, inspired by organizing with people caught up in the criminal punishment system.[22] As Erica Perry of the Black Nashville Assembly puts it, "Because we were led by people who are directly impacted, we were forced to look at what it looks like to be taken into custody by police, be put in a cage because you can't afford bail, and then put in front of court for an arraignment in front of an anti-Black prosecutor and judge. We were able to organize people around their rage around their experiences with the police, inside the jail, and inside the courts."[23]

The campaign specifically targets specialized courts such as drug court, veterans' court, and domestic violence court. Perry describes these programs as "coopting our language around wanting people to have access to services instead of incarceration by saying 'we want people to have services so we want to arrest people and force them to access social services they have to pay for in order not to be convicted.'" Black Nashville Assembly developed a survey it distributed in the community asking people where they wanted to take money from in the city budget, and where they wanted to invest it. Many people wanted to take funding from police, courts and jails and invest it in other resources like community-led harm prevention and transformative justice. BNA will now use the information gathered from the survey in prosecutor and judicial elections to question candidates on whether they are willing to meet those demands, and as a part of their invest/divest campaign to shrink the size and power of local courts and the DA's office.

Seattle's Solidarity Budget offers another example of a comprehensive approach to defund campaigns.[24] Angélica Cházaro grounds this approach in a 2016 fight to stop construction of a youth jail, which in turn required reduction of juvenile prosecutions: "if we are not going to have youth incarceration, we also shouldn't have youth adjudication—we can use fights to close or stop jails to push folks toward the inevitable conclusion that we don't need any parts of this system."[25] As Cházaro underscores, ending youth incarceration and all incarceration means ending prosecution too.

In 2020, the Seattle Solidarity Budget coalition initially called for defunding the Seattle Police Department by 50 percent, and worked with the local public defenders to put forth an ordinance in the Seattle Municipal Code to curb the criminalization of behavior related to unmet mental health needs, poverty, and drug use.[26] Cházaro points out that this demand met the greatest resistance: Seattle politicians and business groups seemed less opposed to reducing resources to police than curbing misdemeanor prosecutions and defunding municipal courts.

Nonetheless, in its second year, the Seattle Solidarity Budget broadened its demands, and also called for a 50 percent cut to funding for the criminal divisions of the City Attorney's office and the Seattle Municipal

Court. The City Attorney's Office prosecutes misdemeanors in municipal court where poor people are targeted, hidden, and dehumanized. In addition, the Solidarity Budget campaign demanded the decriminalization of misdemeanor offenses. In their budget proposal, the campaign rejected the municipal court's justification for increased funding and power based on offering alternatives to incarceration for misdemeanor offenses.[27] "Courts and prosecutors are not social service agencies, and should not be the gateway to housing and treatment. Just as responses to mental health crises belong in community hands ... courts and prosecutors should not be funded to provide the basic support and programming people need."

The Seattle Solidarity budget includes: demands to use the resources currently funneled into municipal court to create workgroups of community members and stakeholders to develop alternatives to misdemeanor prosecutions, including misdemeanor domestic violence cases, which currently account for a third of municipal court costs, and to develop a 5-year plan to end municipal court prosecutions in Seattle. These efforts include developing a just transition for court workers, many of whom, including probation and parole workers, are Black, Indigenous or people of color in union jobs.[28] Organizers have begun to make inroads with unions representing court workers by asking "What is it you like about your job? Wouldn't it be great to be able to do the things you want to do for your community in ways that are not based on violence or the threat of violence?"

Deploying Strategies to Defund Courts in Your Community in Your Community

At the heart of organizing that aims to defund carceral institutions community efforts to reimagine public safety and public spending. In Seattle, Nashville and other cities, organizers have developed their own proposal for budgets that would create greater safety for all.

Budgets are reflections of community values and priorities. What governments decide to fund and what they decide not fund are deeply political decisions that are ripe for contestation. For organizers, conversations around budgets are an opportunity to invite community members to reimagine our public institutions and to create the kind of world people need and deserve.

Organizers are working to expose how much their city, county and state spend to operate their criminal courts and offering alternative proposals for allocating those funds. In Seattle, organizers have trained their eyes on municipal court. They have started by working to eliminate the kinds of criminal prosecutions many people agree are harmful and wasteful. But critically, they have not just focused on these types of offenses. For example, they have also won funding for a working group that can help make the case to the public and city council that even instances of domestic violence are best addressed outside of criminal court. In order to accomplish this, organizers are not only identifying how to divest, but also how to invest in community care to truly address the sources of harm.

Social Movement Support Lab has already developed a sophisticated tool to uncover how much your jurisdiction spends on policing, courts, and prisons.[29] You can supplement this data with local information about how much criminal courts cost in your community. For example, check out the cost breakdown for one courtroom in Brooklyn, NY where arraignments take place. Our estimates are modest. We only include the lowest salary ranges and do not include other forms of benefits and payments employees may receive. We only count the people physically inside the courtroom. It takes many more police officers, prosecutors, court officers, lawyers to bring a case from arrest to arraignment, but here is a snapshot.

As you consider a #DefundCopsCourtsandCages or #DefundDA campaign in your community, here are some questions to consider:

- ☞ How could the money currently allocated to pay prosecutors, judges, court officers, police officers and correctional officers be better spent? What would be better ways to put our collective energy and resources to use?

- ☞ As we push to shrink the size, scope and power of courts and its carceral agencies, how can we protect individuals currently navigating courts and prosecutions? What kind of backlash can we anticipate and how can we defend against it?

- ☞ How can we build alliances across movements to demand budgets that deliver comprehensive and inclusive prosperity and safety for us all?

The Cost of Criminal Courts

Organizers across the U.S. are working to expose how much their city, county and state spend to operate their criminal courts and are offering alternative proposals for allocating those funds. That's because budgets are reflections of community values and priorities. What governments decide to fund and what they decide not fund are deeply political decisions that are ripe for contestation. For organizers, conversations around budgets are an opportunity to invite community members to reimagine our public institutions and to create the kind of world people need and deserve.

On the following page, we have collected information about how much New York City and New York State spends to keep a single criminal courtroom running in Brooklyn, specifically the court room where arraignments take place. Our estimates are conservative and underinclusive. It takes many more people to keep the system running, but we only focus on the people in a single physical court room. As you consider the sums of money currently allocated to pay prosecutors, judges, court officers police officers and correction officers, what else could we do with all that money?

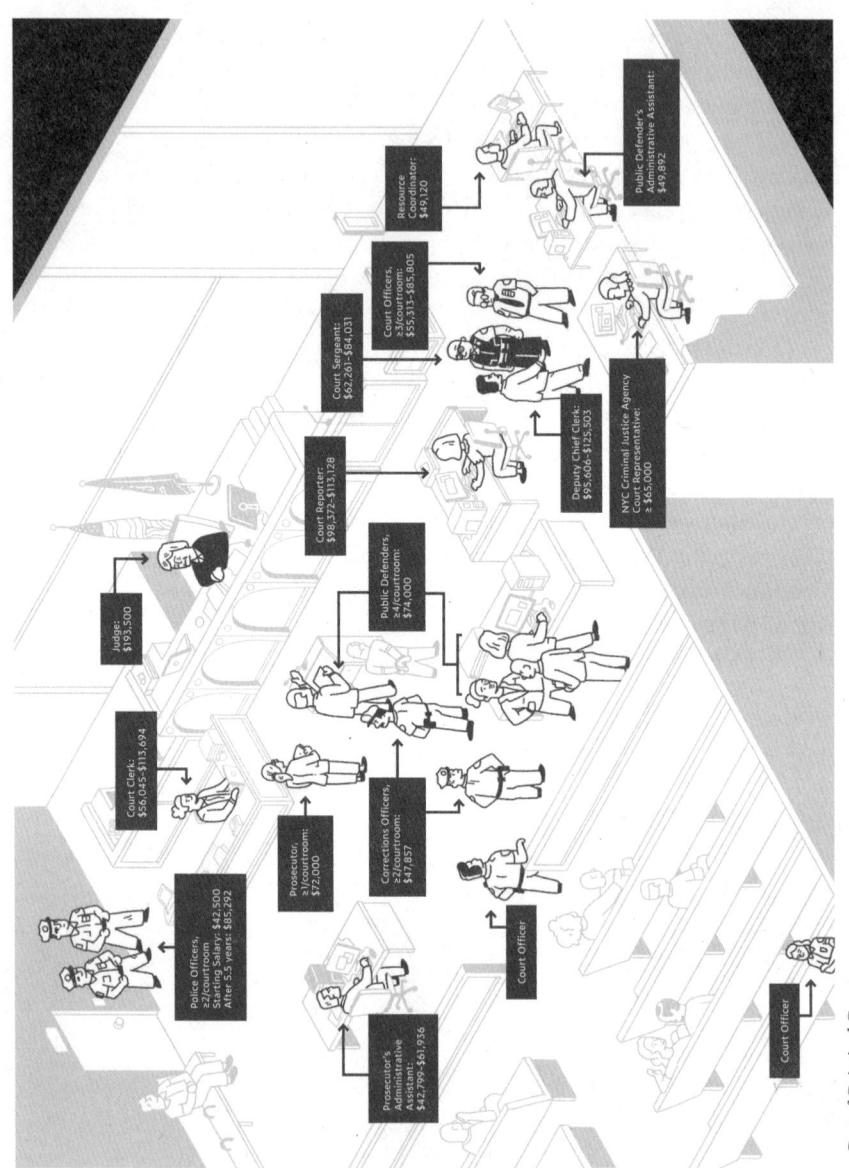

The Cost of Criminal Courts

6

No Such Thing As Progressive Prosecutors

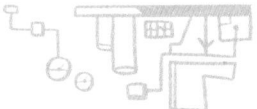

Prosecutors have a lot of power in the criminal punishment system. For this reason, over the past decade in particular, advocates, organizers, journalists, funders and more have pointed to the prosecuting office as a primary site to push for decarceration. Many who approach the criminal punishment system as something that is broken and therefore can be fixed (let's call them "reformists"), have taken up a candidate-focused electoral strategy that seeks to elect so-called "progressive prosecutors," candidates who promise to implement a series of decarceral reforms once in office. We put the term "progressive prosecutors" in quotation marks because, as abolitionists, we understand prosecution to be a systemic component of the criminal punishment system,[1] a death-making system of racialized social control that cannot be progressive, no matter the personal politics of the individual person in office.[2]

Besides being an oxymoron, law professor Benjamin Levin has written about how the term "progressive prosecutor" is a category that has no meaning, a term that "means many different things to many different people."[3] We agree, and yet there are several prosecutors who have been elected in the last five years who have been nationally recognized by media,[4] non-profits,[5] journalists,[6] funders,[7] voters,[8] and especially themselves[9] as "progressive," "reform-minded," or "decarceral" prosecutors. These prosecutors include, but are not limited to, Philadelphia District Attorney (DA) Larry Krasner, Chicago State's Attorney Kim Foxx, Brooklyn DA Eric Gonzalez, Baltimore State's Attorney Marilyn Mosby, Boston DA Rachael Rollins, and San Francisco DA Chesa Boudin. All of these individuals are members of the non-profit organization and prosecutor network: "Fair and Just Prosecution."[10]

The "progressive prosecutor" strategy seeks to change the person who is in power, but does not seek to upend the power structure itself. In this piece, we will provide examples of how the individual prosecutors who were elected under this mantle of reform have, in fact, further solidified the power structure of the criminal punishment system by expanding the resources, size, scope, and legitimacy of the prosecuting office. We argue that this is the very point of the reforms: to further entrench the prosecuting office, not destroy it. This piece is an invitation to pursue other organizing strategies that get us closer to our goal of a world without prosecution and therefore without prosecutors.

Admittedly, some of these prosecutors have instituted policies around charging or bail requests that may have contributed to decarceration in their jurisdictions. Fewer people in cages is an important step on the road to an abolitionist future with no people in cages or under any form of carceral control. However, decarceration is not consistently tracked by these offices and in many places, the release of some people (often people charged with less serious charges) allows for the doubling down on the detention of others. For example in Boston[11] and Philadelphia,[12] there have been increases in prosecutor requests for exorbitantly high bail or pretrial detention without the possibility of release, particularly for gun-related offenses, often cementing the racial disparities these prosecutors campaigned against. During the early height of the COVID-19 pandemic, despite making performative pledges to reduce pretrial incarceration, the head prosecutors in Philadelphia, Baltimore, and Chicago continued to request high money bail, to request people be jailed without option for release, and to contest money bail reductions.[13] And regardless, decarceration is not the only metric. By design, the strategy of electing prosecutors with different ideological views does not diminish prosecutorial power over people, even if individual prosecutors choose not to use their power to charge or jail someone. Their successor, after all, could make the opposite choice.

Expanding Size & Resources of Prosecuting Office

One way to measure power is money. Prosecuting offices, like all aspects of law enforcement, are exorbitantly funded. This remains true for all prosecuting offices, regardless of who is at the head of the office. No prosecutor who ran a campaign on the promise to be less carceral has requested a reduction in their budget. In most cases, their budgets have increased (and in the rare cases when they did remain constant or decreased, it was due to overall city or state budget constraints, most recently due to the COVID pandemic). For example, in his proposed 2021 budget, Philadelphia District Attorney Larry Krasner proposed an over $43 million budget, up 11% over his 2020 budget, to pay for new positions and initiatives. However, when the Philadelphia Mayor came out with the city budget, it included a reduction in the District Attorney's budget to $33.3 million (a 14% reduction from 2020), which DA Kranser pleaded with the City Council to reject.[14] In other cities with prosecutors elected promising reforms, like Brooklyn[15] and Boston,[16] even with the pandemic, the prosecuting office's funding increased. And in Baltimore, since Marilyn Mosby was elected State's Attorney in 2015, the State's Attorney's Office budget has increased by a whopping 35 percent.[17]

Often the budget increase requests are for hiring more staff, and therefore to increase the size of the prosecuting office, but also somewhat unique to these prosecutors, the increased funding is often also justified in order to institute "reforms." For example, besides hiring new staff, Philadelphia DA Krasner said increased funding in 2021 was needed to ensure the effectiveness for a new anti-gun violence initiative, as well as to have more resources to investigate "police abuse."[18] In the name of "transparency" and "accountability," DA Krasner's office also received $4.5 million from private philanthropy foundations Arnold Ventures and the Chan Zuckerberg Initiative to study "the short- and long-term impacts of prosecutorial decision-making on individuals, families, and communities in Philadelphia."[19] Philanthropic support has become common[20] over the last few years to both directly fund district attorney offices, as well as organizations that support them, as part of the effort to "transform prosecution."[21] The San Francisco District Attorney office under Chesa Boudin received an increased budget by over $6 million for 2022, and "plans to use resources to reduce racial disparities in prosecution and expand diversionary programs as an alternative to incarceration."[22] These prosecutors do not wish to shrink the office or prosecution, but rather to enlarge their staffing and power in order to implement new programs. Not only do these prosecutors continue prosecuting people, and by definition put people in cages, they also implement other programs and staffing in order to increase the reach of the prosecutor office. These changes are antithetical to abolitionist reform: The measure of abolitionist change is less power and control, not more.

Expanding Scope & Reach of the Prosecuting Office

Establishing and expanding diversion programs are one of the key ways prosecutors not only justify increased budgets, but also expand the scope and reach of the prosecuting office into service-provision. This typically occurs in the realm of nonprofits, hospitals, and community-based organizations. Prosecutorial diversion often works like this: for certain cases (typically for charges that do not carry long jail sentences), the prosecutor will offer the person facing prosecution the opportunity to complete some kind of program, such as mental health treatment, therapy, drug treatment, or in the case of the Brooklyn DA, an art class.[23] If they are able to complete the program successfully, the prosecutor will dismiss or reduce the charges against them. However, if there are any hiccups in completing the program, the prosecutor and the court retain authority to send the person to jail not only for the underlying and still-pending criminal charge(s), but also for breaching their conditions of release. These programs often happen in partnership with non-profits or community-based groups. For example, sometimes the prosecuting offices are funding the programs at non-profits (like in Philadelphia[24] and Boston[25]), sometimes the services at the community organizations are under the supervision and control of the prosecuting office, or sometimes the services can only be delivered with the permission of the prosecuting office.[26] These programs may seem benign, even positive, especially in cases where people successfully complete the program and avoid prosecution. However, what is also true, and by design in such a system, is that prosecutors–and the criminal punishment system more generally–not only now have power over whether or not someone is charged and prosecuted, but also whether they receive access to services and/or treatment. Further, they retain new power to punish in the absence of perfect compliance, whether "failure" to complete the program is willful or not. In other words, the reach of prosecuting offices also extends into neighborhoods and communities, all under the guise of "care" or "support."

Increasing the Legitimacy of the Prosecuting Office

This proximity to "care," "support," and "services" also increases the legitimacy of the prosecuting office as an institution that can deliver safety and healing, and obscures the core purpose of prosecuting offices, which is to punish. Another example of this is San Francisco DA Chesa Boudin, whose office partnered with Lyft[27] and with AirBnB[28] to provide transportation and housing for survivors of domestic violence. These initiatives received applause from domestic violence organizations and the public, directing attention away from the choice the prosecuting office made to support and partner with private companies (who are notoriously anti-labor and contribute to gentrification, rather than advocate for funding to go directly to survivors themselves, to non-carceral anti-violence organizations, to affordable housing or to public transportation. It is a move that undermines public funding and infrastructure, while also cementing the power of the prosecuting office over survivors of domestic violence and strengthening the office's legitimacy as survivor-centered.

Diversion programs and other reforms—whether reducing racial disparities in prosecutions, or diversifying staff of the prosecuting office, or increasing investigations of police officers in individual, sensationalized cases—all contribute to the legitimacy of the prosecuting office. They are public relations strategies aimed at softening the prosecuting office's image, while continuing the machinery of criminal punishment under both new and old structures. They cement the idea that prosecuting offices, with just a few tweaks here and there, are necessary for ensuring justice, fairness, and safety. After the summer 2020 uprisings for Black liberation and against policing, Chesa Boudin, Rachael Rollins, and Larry Krasner (the DAs in San Francisco, Boston, and Philadelphia, respectively) came together with Shaun King's Grassroots Law Project (which is affiliated with a PAC that had supported many of their campaigns) and pledged to start Truth Justice and Reconciliation Commissions about police violence in their cities. In a moment of insurgency, as an insidious way to regain legitimacy, power and control, these prosecutors and some of their most prominent funders co-opted the language of movements in order to perpetuate and strengthen the myth that prosecutors can provide safety, justice, or reconciliation.[29]

Despite co-opting social movement language, one of the other ways these prosecutors bolster the legitimacy and necessity of prosecuting offices is by attacking and defacing organizers and movement organizations. Baltimore DA Marilyn Mosby, who as of July 2022 has tried to convict Keith Davis Jr. for murder unsuccessfully four different times[30] and was pursuing charges for a fifth time, was caught on video giving the middle finger to a bicyclist who rode past her while shouting, "Free Keith Davis Jr.!" On Democracy Now, Philadelphia District Attorney Larry Krasner used fear-mongering and racist language to claim that by posting bail for people who could not afford it, the Philadelphia Community Bail Fund was allowing harm to happen in the community.[31] Importantly, this stoking of fear also justified his office's practice of routinely requesting exorbitant, million dollar money bails for Philadelphians who could never afford that price tag on their freedom. A very similar story transpired with Suffolk County District Attorney Rachael Rollins and the Massachusetts Bail Fund.[32] Like all prosecutors, the prosecutors elected promising decarceration still believe in and sustain the idea that police and prosecutions are necessary to keep communities safe.

Prosecutors Cannot End "Mass Incarceration." Abolition Now.

One of the ways the "progressive prosecutor" strategy was sold to voters, by the candidates themselves and their supporters, was that by substituting a "tough-on-crime" prosecutor with a "progressive" or "decarceral" prosecutor, we could "end mass incarceration." But that was a lie. Prosecutors are key drivers of incarceration, but as individuals they cannot undo decades of systemic hyper-criminalization and incarceration. Across the country, "progressive prosecutors'"reforms have been blocked or disrupted by their own staff,[33] judges,[34] legislators,[35] cops,[36] governors[37] and all of the above.[38] Now, it seems, we must also elect "progressive" judges and sheriffs to really "end mass incarceration." Do we though? Or is it more accurate to recognize that "the whole damn system is guilty as hell"[39] and, no matter who holds the different positions, the structural design to control and punish remains the same.

Prosecution is just one component of a system that is designed to punish; a system that is rooted in and upheld by white supremacy, racial capitalism, and colonial conquest. Prosecution cannot function without policing, without the courts, without the law and procedure–targeting one component without understanding their interconnectedness as part of a racist and violent system leads to a never ending game of trying to whack-a-mole your way to change.

When we look at the above examples of what the elected prosecutors who promised reforms have done while in office, it is clear that they have only found new ways to expand the resources, size, scope, legitimacy–and therefore power–of their offices. When people running for the office responsible for prosecuting people felt it was politically advantageous to claim they would be more "fair and just," they did so without giving up any power and control over the community. Whether you are "tough on crime" or "progressive" or "community minded" it is largely irrelevant if you seek to prop up the power of the office, expand your power and control over people and communities being prosecuted, and increase staffing and budget.

Fortunately, a candidate-focused electoral strategy is not the only way to target the prosecuting office. There are other organizing strategies that align with abolitionist principles and that do not further entrench the power of the prosecuting office. Whether organizing for the decriminalization of sex work or to defund prosecuting office's budgets, there are tangible steps to take that do shrink the power, size, scope, and resources of the prosecuting office and the entire criminal punishment system. See the next chapter, "Abolitionist Principles and Campaign Strategies for Prosecutor Organizing," for more concrete ideas. These are the kinds of steps we can take as we build the power necessary to make a future without prosecution, policing, and prisons possible.

7

Abolitionist Principles & Campaign Strategies for Prosecutor Organizing

As prison abolitionists, we are fighting for a world where the response to social problems does not include prisons, policing, prosecution, or any form of surveillance, supervision, or incarceration. These systems of punishment rely on, reinforce, and perpetuate structures of oppression: white supremacy, patriarchy, capitalism, xenophobia, ableism, and heterosexism. We aim to abolish these systems, not reform them.

As abolitionists, we envision a future without prosecutors and prosecution. Simply put, that is our orientation to prosecutor organizing. We focus on structural and systemic changes that lessen the power, size, and scope of the prosecuting office, and on running campaigns that build the power, size and strength of abolitionist movements.

In most jurisdictions, prosecutors are elected officials tasked with distributing punishment within an unequal and violent society. Just like electing any elected official, electing a new prosecutor, even as part of a larger strategy, is never the end goal because it does not disrupt the existence of the prosecuting office or end the violence of criminalization. We believe that organizations engaged in prosecutor-focused electoral politics must be committed to base-building and accountable to communities most impacted by prosecution and mass criminalization.

As abolitionists, our job does not end with the election of any prosecutor, no matter what they claim to represent. Therefore, we reject the ten-
dency toward cults of personality. We focus on what policies a prosecuting
office enacts and supports others in enacting, what decisions a prosecuting
office makes to release people from the grips of mass criminalization, and
how a prosecuting office relates to, impedes, or advances our movements'
demands. Our organizing focuses on how a prosecuting office's policies
and practices result in decriminalization, decarceration, and shrinking the
resources and power of the office of the prosecutor. Elected prosecutors
are not co-strugglers, but targets we can push on the path to eliminating
prosecution altogether.

The following is a framework that seeks to draw out what "prosecutor
organizing" looks like with an abolitionist lens. The first section outlines
principles to hold us accountable to each other, so that there is shared agreement about what abolition means in organizing around prosecutors. The
second section is a resource for organizers looking to put these principles
into practice in their local prosecutor organizing campaigns.

What do we believe?
Abolitionist Principles for Prosecutor Organizing

o   **Prosecutors are law enforcement: they send people to pris-
    on and jail, parole and probation.** A commitment to abolition
    includes the abolition of prosecutors, surveillance, and policing.
    This means that we seek the abolition of the role of prosecutor
    within the criminal punishment system.

o   **Prosecution is a systemic and structural component of the
    criminal punishment system.** Discussions of "good", "bad", "pro-
    gressive", or "regressive" prosecutors keep the focus on individu-
    als and are a distraction that impedes the need for structural and
    systemic change.

o   **Abolition is opposed to prosecution.** A commitment to abo-
    lition requires that we think outside the criminal punishment
    system for what accountability and healing from harm could

look like. This means we condemn the prosecution of anyone, including police officers, people in positions of power accused of financially-motivated crimes ("white collar crimes"), exploitative landlords, people accused of sexual or interpersonal harm, and so on.

o **Prosecutors are not social workers, therapists, housing advocates, or any other service-oriented role.** They cannot and should not provide services to people who are in need. This is inherently in conflict with their pledge to serve and maintain the criminal punishment system. The best thing prosecutors can do for people who need services is get out of the way. Prosecuting offices should not receive more resources to provide social services or survivor/victim support, nor bolster other forms of confinement, stripping of rights, or institutions that use threat of punishment to force treatment or coerce services (such as drug courts and other forms of diversion court; mental health jailing). Resource shifting from carceral prosecution to carceral social services is not de-resourcing. Social services become another tool of the punishment system whether housed in or mandated by the prosecuting office. Giving more resources to death-making institutions is not abolitionist. It only cements and increases power and also cloaks the system in legitimacy. Instead, prosecutors should advocate for resources to be distributed to community organizations that already provide services and for policies that redistribute resources.

o **Prosecuting offices cannot be "co-governed" with/by community organizations.** Given the inherent power imbalance, there is no shared power relationship between elected prosecutors and community organizations. Instead, community organizations are constituency organizations and can and should demand change from these elected officials within that relationship. This means using the tools of community accountability including phone calls, constituent meetings, protests, and the same demands we make of every and any elected official.

o **Prosecuting offices must be stripped of power and resources.** Even as they restructure their offices and review prosecutions handled by their predecessor(s), prosecutors should not seek additional resources but work to redistribute resources internally to shrink the scale of current and future prosecutions as well as redress histories of aggressive prosecutions.

How do we get there?
Developing local organizing campaigns on the road to abolition

As abolitionists, we are working towards a future where people are no longer prosecuted and therefore where prosecutors do not exist. That future is a long way off. To get there, our movements need to build significant power through a variety of organizing interventions while remaining pointedly focused on shrinking the power, size, and scope of the prosecuting office.

There is not one path to abolishing prosecutors. But there certainly are identifiable strategies and tactics on the long road to making prosecutors obsolete. Some may be exercised concurrently, others sequentially. As we engage in abolitionist struggle and experimentation, we will together identify new strategies and possibilities in the transformed landscape. Where your local organizing can intervene in this continuum will depend on your capacity, how much power you have already built, and your local political context.

Tactics and Strategies Toward Abolishing Prosecutors

Baseline Tactics
Base-building

o   Increase the number of people who share the vision for abolition and who are willing to do the work to move that vision forward. Build your movement, reach out to directly affected people, develop relationships, facilitate leadership development, create internal political education and analysis building, work intentionally in broad and deep coalitions.

o   In order to build the power required to ensure systemic and structural changes, base-building must be continuous throughout all other activities.

Consciousness-raising and narrative-shift

o   Public, political education on the power of prosecutors, the prison industrial complex, criminalization, white supremacy/capitalism/root causes of harm, abolition, transformative justice can come in many forms including:

  ◉   *Hosting teach-ins, workshops, trainings, community discussions, town-halls.*

  ◉   *Organizing Twitter power hours or other social media campaigns anchored in education and sharing resources/materials on these topics.*

o   Develop a media strategy for your campaign that shifts traditional punishment narratives, uses less stigmatizing language, fights the victim/perpetrator binary, and rejects "public safety" framing to focus on what communities say they need to thrive.

o   In order to build the power required to ensure systemic and structural changes, narrative shift and public education must be continuous throughout all other activities. The system will react to actions that shift power and so the need for narrative and message definition and consciousness raising will be continuous.

Mutual Aid projects as organizing interventions

o   Mutual Aid is "a form of political participation in which people
    take responsibility for caring for one another and changing politi-
    cal conditions, not just through symbolic acts or putting pressure
    on their representatives in government, but by actually building
    new social relations that are more survivable."[1] Our movements
    currently engage in many forms of mutual aid as both harm reduc-
    tion and steps towards abolitionist organizing including:

    ⊙   *Community bail funds and targeted bail-out actions that free peo-
        ple from incarceration and lift up data and experience to push
        for change.*

    ⊙   *Participatory defense organizing that gets families to use their
        power as community to win freedom, make strong bail arguments
        for release and fight back against DA requests, offer alternative
        diversion plans, initiate plea negotiations with true diversion
        and alternatives, and fill courtrooms to demonstrate community
        support.*

    ⊙   *Post-release community support projects that establish commu-
        nity-based services to assist individuals upon release and model
        non-carceral examples.*

o   In order to build the power required to ensure systemic and struc-
    tural changes, mutual aid and organizing interventions must be
    connected to a larger organizing strategy and part of a theory of
    change.[2]

Strategies Focused on the Prosecuting Office
Electoral Organizing

o   Organize to remove officeholders and staff in the prosecuting of-
    fice committed to status quo punishment and harm. Opposition
    is an abolitionist harm reduction strategy. While this focuses on
    firing individuals in the interim, the orientation is always on the
    systemic and structural and abolitionist organizers must consis-
    tently uplift this point in public. Opposition efforts can be de-
    ployed in different ways including:

◎ *Elections focused on removing an office holder (without a partic-ular candidate for support).*

◎ *Recall elections.*

◎ *Forcing resignation (often via investigation and hearings).*

o Organize to elect candidates who make commitments to policy changes that are decarceral and reduce their office's harm, power, and influence.

◎ *In general, election season can be a good opportunity for abolition-ist base building, if information being distributed is issue-focused and not candidate-focused. Organizers can conduct issue-based canvassing and public education forums about the role of the elect-ed prosecutor in the criminal punishment system.*

◎ *Continue reading for considerations in crafting demands, as well as example demands.*

Shifting Office Policy and Culture

o Hold elected prosecutors accountable to implementing promised policy changes. Design and demand new policy changes, beyond those promised during the campaign.

◎ *Tracking implementation of policy change, especially when there is a written office memo or new proposed practice, is relatively clear cut. Tactics include data monitoring, courtwatching, etc.*

◎ *Continue reading for example demands around data transpar-ency and the kinds of data that prosecuting offices should release. Prosecuting offices should not get any more money or resources to track, manage, or release data. The demand should be that they reallocate resources internally to solve this problem.*

◎ *Monitor existing gains while also advocating for even more de-carceral shifts or changes to other harmful practices.*

o Ensure elected prosecutors institute culture change within the prosecuting office.

◎ *Culture change is difficult to organize around because it's more diffuse. Tactics include getting DAs to make personnel changes, restructure their office (like charging units, post-conviction units), require extensive re-training, etc.*

- ◉ *This will require more community power and likely insider tactics.*
- ◉ *Recognize that office policy influences culture, and office culture influences policy.*

Strategies Focused on Shrinking Structural Power
Shrinking Systems of Harm

- ○ Design, demand, and implement abolitionist policies to reduce the reach and influence of the prosecutor. Win structural and systemic change that decreases the size, scope, and power of the prosecuting office in a material and sustainable way.

  - ◉ *This necessarily requires legal change outside the prosecuting office itself: in other words, for local, state, and federal legislation that will strip power, resources, staff, and money from prosecuting offices, in a way that a new prosecutor cannot easily undermine.*
  - ◉ *This could also look like repealing laws that criminalize behavior, reducing prosecutorial discretion in plea bargaining, and fighting against new criminal laws, enhanced penalties, etc.*
  - ◉ *Continue reading for considerations in choosing your targets.*

- ○ Pressure other criminal punishment system stakeholders (judges, police, public defenders, court administrators) to make decarceral and de-resourcing changes. Prosecutors have immense power, but they are also only one piece of a violent, punitive ecosystem.

  - ◉ *This is multi-layered: (1) ensure other stakeholders do not block prosecutors when prosecutors are trying to enact decarceral reforms; (2) ensure other stakeholders do not evade or adapt around prosecutor reforms so the reforms are unable to go into effect; (3) ensure other stakeholders use their influence to support prosecutors in enacting decarceral reforms; (4) ensure other stakeholders adopt their own decarceral and de-resourcing reforms.*

Boosting Resources for Community

- ○ Pressure state and local actors to prioritize funding for community-based resources that produce safety and well-being, such as education, health care, affordable housing, and employment. Simultaneously pressure state and local actors to well as reduce spending for all state systems connected to arms of the criminal punishment system, such as prosecutors, police, court system.

Questions for organizers to consider
in crafting their campaigns

Things to consider when creating your demands:

o   How do your demands delegitimize the prosecuting office? How do your demands limit the power, staff, technology, and resources of the prosecuting office? How do your demands challenge the notion that prosecutors promote safety?

o   Do your demands help our movements build power long term? How do your demands build power for our movements and our people over the long term? To whom are we accountable?

o   Do your demands prioritize people facing more or less serious charges? How do demands focusing on non-serious non-violent charges make it harder to free everyone else?

o   How do your demands take into account an attempt to free the highest numbers of people, while also prioritizing freeing the people who are the most criminalized and demonized and scapegoated, while also prioritizing freeing the people the system harms disproportionately?

o   Do your demands primarily rely on the prosecutor using their individual discretionary power or do they require change to the office in more material, sustainable ways? Do your demands call for strategic deployment of resources by the prosecuting office that ultimately reinforce the power of the prosecutor?

  ⦿   *For example, demanding prosecutors decline to prosecute certain charges is a discretionary decision that depends on the particular prosecutor in power (and follow-through by individual line pros-*

ecutors). By contrast, successfully demanding prosecutors support repealing laws that criminalize behavior would result in legislative change that could not be as easily reversed with the election of a different prosecutor.

o   Do your demands support the provision of rights or services to one person or group of people contingent on the criminalization of another person or group of people?

Things to consider when choosing your targets:

o   Do a power mapping of your place. Who funds the prosecuting office in your jurisdiction? Who do they answer to?

o   Who else can we pressure to downsize the office of the prosecutor?

o   Are other local policymakers likely to be more or less hostile to your goals? How can that inform your strategy? ·

o   Are there decision points where the prosecutor does not answer to anyone else? How can you shape demands that target those decisions? For example, in most jurisdictions, prosecutors can use a particular type of motion to decline charges without requiring approval from a judge.

o   What is the relationship between the prosecuting office and other actors in the criminal punishment system? Does the chief prosecutor have oversight over police detective promotions or hiring decisions in certain units? Are there policies or personnel decisions where a change in the prosecuting office will have a direct effect on curbing or shifting the practices or policies of other related but insulated institutions, like the police?

o   What other actors in the criminal punishment system and beyond may stand in the way of change? How can your organizing antici-pate and respond to pushback from police, judges and court staff, probation and parole officers, local media, other elected officials, and police and corrections workers' unions?

Example Demands

Organizers should conduct a power analysis of their place and context and consider the questions above when crafting demands and deciding on targets. Here are some example demands, grouped into broad categories. They are not exhaustive, and we hope they spark ideas specific to your local context.

o **De-resource.** Demand reduced budgets, staff, and scope of power (including curtailing prosecutorial discretion).

o **De-criminalize.** Demand that prosecutors never initiate or support the creation of new laws criminalizing more behavior. Advocate for current laws to be repealed. Demand (retroactive) sentencing reforms to eliminate mandatory minimums, reduce maximums, and eliminate sentencing enhancements.

o **Stop the prosecution and punishment machine.** Demand that fewer people are prosecuted or subject to detention or detention-like conditions, such as jail, prison, e-carceration (GPS shackles/electronic monitoring), immigration prison, deportation, stay away orders, and supervision (pre-trial, probation, parole). Demand an end to stacking charges, up-charging, and plea bargaining. Demand an end to the practice of requesting bail: affirmatively recommend pre-trial freedom in all cases. Demand an end to requests for detention without bail; warrants for missed court appearances; fines or fees; continuances and case delays. Demand an end to the practice of requesting the death penalty and life sentences with or without parole.

o **Firewalls.** Demand firewalls between prosecuting offices and social service agencies, as well as the police, other law enforcement agencies, hospitals, Department of Children/Family Services, public housing, and any other state or federal investigative agency. When social workers, therapists, and other mandated reporters work in or with a prosecuting office, they become an arm of and accomplice to law enforcement.

o **Fund community.** Demand funding for community organizations supporting people in need. Advocate overall for less government spending on law enforcement, carceral institutions, and other actors in the criminal punishment system and more spending on education, housing, healthcare, community groups, and services that people need to live and be well.

○ **Advocate for access to a meaningful defense.** Demand that prosecutors provide open and early discovery, support funding for public defense, and end the secret grand jury process.

○ **Reject hi-tech interventions that reinforce racism.** Demand that prosecutors reject the use of risk assessment algorithm tools (RATs), race-blind prosecution, or other technological solutions that tinker at the margins of systemic harm and pretend that color-blind interventions can repair a system built on racialized and class-based social control.

○ **Reduce past harm.** Demand that prosecutors reduce harms of prior prosecutions via conviction review and sentencing reductions, vacatur motions, supporting clemency and parole (including medical parole, elder parole, compassionate release), and discharge/grants of liberty for pregnant women. Fundamentally change the approach to appeals; support motions for DNA testing; move to reduce and end terms of supervision on probation and parole.

○ **De-platform.** Reject and disrupt media narratives that use individual cases to laud the role of the prosecutor and obscure the daily grind of prosecutions. Call out when prosecutors use high profile cases, salacious details, or "violent crimes" to justify the prosecutor's role. Reject when prosecutors position the DA or the system as equipped to solve what society relies on it to do. Demand that people see the system for what it is: a race- and class-based punishment machine.

○ **Transparency.** Demand that prosecutors express and follow through on a commitment to transparency by releasing as much data as possible, as regularly as possible, without more resources. Data allows organizers to monitor the pace of change. Data should showcase both prosecutor behavior (e.g. bail requests, plea offers, sentencing recommendations) and case outcomes (e.g. bail imposed, case resolution, sentence imposed). Public data might include the total number of prosecutions, with the option to disaggregate by case type to track specific policies (declination, felony review, etc.); the number of people held in jail pre-trial; and the number of aggregate years of incarceration in sentencing recommendations and sentences imposed. Can the data be broken down by courtroom? Can prosecutors get access to and publish data from other system actors?

- ◉ *Prosecuting offices should not get any additional funding or resources to track, manage, or release data. Demand that prosecuting offices reallocate resources internally to solve this problem.*

o **Demand changes from other actors.** Demand prosecutors reject abusive policing practices (consent searches, gang raids, gang databases, unconstitutional evidence collection, racial profiling), refuse to use the fruits of those practices in prosecutions, and decline to work with known unreliable officers at all (beyond offering testimony in court).

o **Demand support for closing jails and prisons.** Demand opposition to building new jails or prisons.

o **Supervision and consequences.** Advocate for the end to prosecutorial immunity, through legislation or referendum, and qualified immunity for police. Create legal recourse for wrongfully convicted individuals and directly impacted communities to obtain civil sanctions against prosecutors who violate their rights and public trust. Consider other forms of independent oversight that would not enhance the power of the office of the prosecutor but would create opportunities for disciplinary action for attorneys.

Glossary

Ableism: Ableism is the oppression people and groups to face due to a perceived or lived disability.

Ableism can result in the denial of resources, agency and dignity based on one's abilities, whether mental, intellectual, emotional or physical. As the Anti-Violence Project explains, "Ableism depends on a binary, and benefits able-bodied people at the expense of disabled people. Like other forms of oppression, ableism operates on individual, institutional and cultural levels."[1] Ableism extends to oppression that a person or groups may face on account of the social expectation to be sane, rational, and not neurodivergent or psychiatrically disabled.[2] Ableism, as experienced and structured, is inseparable from racism and classism. As we show in "Criminal Court 101" (Chapter One), individuals endure ableist oppression throughout the criminal process. The law only recognizes a narrow band of disabilities as legitimate and worthy of accommodations, even those can be deeply inadequate and often harmful, leaving many criminalized disabled people abandoned or further controlled.

Alternatives to Incarceration (ATI): ATIs are when a person charged with or convicted of a crime is offered an alternative option instead of incarceration. Participants must successfully complete the ATI program mandates in order to avoid jail or prison and/or to receive reduced criminal sanctions.

Alternatives to incarceration include supervision programs (typically with some element of "treatment," counseling, therapy, or employment/education/housing services), probation, house arrest, location tracking, community service, and fines and restitution. In many cases, whether or not someone is eligible for an ATI is decided by the judge or prosecutor after someone has already been convicted or pled guilty. Although ATIs have been widely embraced, these replace one form of supervision (prison), with another (therapeutic programs), but do not reduce the state's power to criminalize and intervene in people's lives.

Arraignment: The arraignment is the first appearance before a judge, during which a person accused of a crime is notified of and answers the charges against them.

It is the beginning of the criminal case from the court's perspective. In some jurisdictions, a person accused of a crime will have more than one arraignment, once before the grand jury hears the case and once after the grand jury has voted on an indictment. Arraignments are short and impersonal appearances that rarely give the person accused a full picture of the charges against them.

Border Imperialism: Instead of seeing the rush of migrants at borders in the United States and Europe as the source of the crisis, the term border imperialism directs our attention to the border itself as the source of the crisis.

Organizer and author Harsha Walia explains that border imperialism encapsulates four elements: "first, the mass displacement of impoverished and colonized communities resulting from asymmetrical relations of global power, and the simultaneous securitization of the border against those migrants whom capitalism and empire have displaced; second, the criminalization of migration with severe punishment and discipline of those deemed 'alien' or 'illegal'; third, the entrenchment of a racialized hierarchy of citizenship by arbitrating who legitimately constitutes the nation-state; and fourth, the state-mediated exploitation of migrant labor, akin to conditions of slavery and servitude, by capitalist interests."[3]

Bail: Bail is the process for securing release for someone who is charged with a crime while they await trial.

Conditions of bail or release may be imposed, such as an order to not contact someone, avoid a location, not get re-arrested, take weekly drug tests, or not leave the state. The condition that people are usually most familiar with is having to pay money—which is why many people use the term "bail" to specifically refer to money bail. Although the person is technically presumed innocent when bail is set, the courts have the authority to supervise and restrict the accused's freedom.

Cisheteropatriarchy: Cisheteropatriarchy is the oppressive set of assumptions that maintains that the normal expression of sexuality is one of a married couple of two people, male and female, whose gender corresponds with their birth sex.

These views permeate dominant culture and are expressed in everyday discourse, the media, welfare systems, and areas of law, including criminal law. These assumptions are apparent in the moral panics and subsequent attempts to regulate and criminalize a range of sexual practices deemed deviant such as promiscuity, pornography, sex work, one-parent families, and extra-marital sex. It creates the conditions for the criminalization and oppression of queer and trans people specifically.

Criminal Law: Criminal laws define what is a crime: the actions, activities, behaviors or statuses that the state condemns and can punish by limiting a person's freedom or by monetary sanctions, like fines and fees.

Sometimes lower-level offenses*,

like "disorderly conduct" or drinking in public spaces, are characterized as violations rather than crimes because they don't give someone a criminal record. What ends up being considered a crime is the outcome of specific decisions made by legislators about what kinds of conduct to punish, by whom, and how. Those decisions have historically tended to criminalize poor, Black, Indigenous, Latinx, LGBTQ, disabled, migrant, and radical left communities and persons.

A note on the term "lower-level offenses." Colloquially we use this term to refer to charges that societally we think of as being "less serious" or "less violent," we also use this term to refer to charges which we think of as carrying a less severe punishment. It's important to note that those connections are often assumed because of the language used and they do not always mean this legally. Many charges we think of as being "lower-level" carry potentially lengthy prison sentences.

Criminal Procedure: Criminal procedure are the rules of criminal court.

The rules as written tell criminal court actors (judges, prosecutors, probation officers, clerks, and defense attorneys) what they have to do in order for a criminal case to move forward. The rules are written by legislators who have historically given most power to judges and prosecutors, who also have tremendous power to decide how to interpret those rules. Their way of enforcing the rules is just as important as the rules themselves. Criminal procedure tells us what kind of proof the prosecutor needs to provide to justify a charge. It spells out the deadlines prosecutors have to provide the proof. It also dictates the kind of information the defense is entitled to receive to prepare for trial or a plea and what kind of evidence can be produced at trial. Criminal procedure regulates the kinds of behavior, questions, and actions that are permitted or required when prosecuting, defending, or deciding a criminal case. Criminal procedure is the "how" of criminal law.

Diversion: Diversion refers to any formal procedural intervention, led or facilitated by state actors (police, DAs, or judges), that temporarily and conditionally redirects a person's path through the criminal process away from arrest, jail, charges, plea, or conviction in exchange for enrollment and participation in a program ("rehabilitation," "community service," "treatment," or "education," etc.).

Generally, diversion programs must create the possibility of closing a case without a conviction or with a reduced charge (like a misdemeanor instead of a felony). Diversion programs are similar to what courts call

alternatives to incarceration or problem-solving courts, but often diversion programs come with the promise that the charges the prosecutor initially brought will be reduced or dropped.

Grand Jury: The grand jury is a group of people selected from the public to decide together whether the prosecutor has probable cause to pursue charges against a defendant.

The purpose of grand juries is to secure an indictment. Although grand juries are seen as a check on the prosecutor's power, these tend to function like a rubber stamp.

Indictment: An indictment is a formal statement the prosecutor writes charging a person with an offense, substantiated through a grand jury or preliminary hearing determining there is probable cause. The evidence required for an indictment is low–all the prosecutor needs is probable cause.

Judge: The judge's role is to make decisions about requests or arguments about charges, bail, and pre-trial supervision made by the defense or prosecutor.

The judge is supposed to be impartial—not prefer one side over the other. But most judges are former prosecutors and their former experiences inevitably inform their rulings.[4]

In other words, a judge often functions as a second prosecutor.

Jury Nullification: Jury nullification is when jurors (whether as part of a grand jury or trial jury) vote against an indictment or return a 'Not Guilty' verdict even if they believe the accused person has broken the law. Jurors are traditionally not taught about their power to nullify.

Motions: Motions are legal requests the parties make.

In criminal court, the motions filed during court appearances usually concern what evidence the prosecution will be permitted to present at trial. The defense will move to suppress (keep out) certain kinds of evidence the prosecutor may try to introduce, or to prevent the prosecution from using evidence of the defendant's prior convictions. The defense rarely wins on these motions. The defense can also file a motion to ask the judge to dismiss the charges, but that rarely happens. The judge can dismiss the charges if they disagree with the grand jury that there is enough evidence to sustain the charges. The defense can also file a motion to ask the judge to reduce the bail and to order that the prosecution turn over evidence. The judge has decision-making power over motions and the ruling on these mo-

tions will determine how a trial will go.

Plea Bargain: A plea bargain is when the prosecutor allows the defense to plead guilty to a charge less than the maximum charge in exchange for giving up their right to trial.

Over 90 percent of cases are resolved by plea bargains. Prosecutors have all the leverage in plea bargain negotiations.

Preliminary Hearing: The purpose of the preliminary hearing is for a judge or magistrate to decide whether the prosecution has probable cause to pursue the charges against the accused. They are sometimes called probable cause hearings.

Judges are often reluctant to dismiss charges at this stage, and it does not happen frequently.

Preventive Detention: Preventive detention is when an accused person is detained for the duration of their prosecution and no amount of money can secure their freedom. In some states this is referred to as "remand."

Judges imposing and prosecutors seeking preventative detention often make arguments that the person accused is a danger to the community. Preventative detention denies someone their freedom when they are technically presumed to be innocent.

Prison Industrial Complex: As defined by Critical Resistance, "The prison industrial complex (PIC) is a term we use to describe the overlapping interests of government and industry that use surveillance, policing, and imprisonment as solutions to economic, social and political problems.

Through its reach and impact, the PIC helps and maintains the authority of people who get their power through racial, economic and other privileges. There are many ways this power is collected and maintained through the PIC, including creating mass media images that keep alive stereotypes of people of color, poor people, queer people, immigrants, youth, and other oppressed communities as criminal, delinquent, or deviant. This power is also maintained by earning huge profits for private companies that deal with prisons and police forces; helping earn political gains for "tough on crime" politicians; increasing the influence of prison guard and police unions; and eliminating social and political dissent by oppressed communities that make demands for self-determination and reorganization of power in the U.S."

Probable Cause: To determine probable cause, courts ask whether a person of reasonable caution believes that a crime has been committed, supported by specific objective facts. There's not much more guidance than this general statement, but it is intended to be a low burden of proof.

The amount of evidence required for probable cause is not clearly defined. Here are some examples: The police cannot arrest someone just because they don't like the way a person looks, but if, for example, they see someone running in an area the police say is a "high crime area" with a bulge in their pocket, the police could stop, and search that person—and that usually is enough probable cause for an arrest. Before a grand jury, if a witness can describe a person engaging in a criminal act and they seem credible, that is usually enough for probable cause for an indictment. The witness does not need to bring video surveillance, or medical records. A single witness is enough.

Probation Hold: A probation hold renders someone ineligible for release until the judge determines, through a separate hearing, whether the terms of their probation have been violated and probation should be revoked. This is also sometimes called a "detainer."

Something similar can happen when someone is on parole and is re-arrested. This is often called a "parole hold."

Problem-Solving Courts: Problem-solving courts are specialized criminal courts that offer enhanced supervision and "treatment" in addition to or in lieu of incarceration.

Oftentimes, the person being prosecuted needs to plead guilty to the top charge and then if they complete the program successfully, the conviction will be eligible for expungement (although this doesn't always occur in practice).[5] There are many kinds of problem- solving courts but they generally fall into three categories: (1) "treatment" courts, such as mental health courts and drug courts; (2) offense-specific courts, such as domestic violence courts and community courts; and (3) status courts, such as veterans courts and homelessness courts. As law professor, Erin Collins explains, "Despite this diversity, the universe of problem-solving courts is united by a common claim, namely, that these courts solve a problem that would otherwise lead to repeated interaction with the criminal legal system."[6] As with alternatives to incarceration, problem solving courts preserve the state's power to criminalize, but do it in new, and seemingly less offensive ways than incarceration.

Prosecutors: Prosecutors, often called District Attorneys or State's Attorneys, are lawyers for the government. They hold the power to decide who is charged with a crime, whether to prosecute someone at all, what charges to file, whether to request bail and how much, and whether to enter into a plea agreement. This is called "prosecutorial discretion."

In many places, the head District or State Attorney is an elected position, and this elected official then supervises a team of hired prosecutors (often called Assistant District Attorneys or ADAs) who actually handle most of the cases in criminal court. In a few states, like Connecticut, Alaska, and New Jersey, the head prosecutor is appointed, not elected. Prosecutors are one of the most powerful actors in criminal court.

Public Defenders: Public defenders are defense lawyers paid for by the state to represent accused people who cannot afford legal assistance.

Just because they are paid by the government doesn't mean they are on the government's side–lots of public defenders are very skilled and deeply committed to their clients' rights and freedoms. The quality of the representation and when you get a lawyer varies across jurisdictions and depends on the resources available. Not every state has an organization dedicated to representing low-income people accused of crimes. In those states, attorneys are appointed on a case-by-case basis. And, even in places with dedicated public defender agencies, the agencies are notoriously underfunded and overworked, with annual caseloads spanning from 50-590 cases per public defender.[7]

Racial Capitalism: As geographer and organizer Ruth Wilson Gilmore has said, "Capitalism requires inequality and racism enshrines it...All capitalism is racial from its beginning, which is to say the capitalism that we have inherited is constantly and reproducing itself and it will continue to depend on racial practice and racial hierarchy. No matter what."[8]

Capitalism requires a division of labor and power. There are those who own and profit from the factories, the land, the intellectual property and the companies, and there are those whose labor is exploited to produce value that keeps the economy going. One of the ways our society differentiates between these roles and preserves the power of the capital owning class is by justifying these differences as racial hierarchies. Groups of people are classified based on real or imagined attributes and their lives are devalued on account of these traits. Criminalization is a tool the state uses to manage those discarded by racial capitalism, and reinforces race and class based hierarchies by marking people with criminal records and depriving them of life chances.

Speedy Trial: Speedy trial is the con-stitutional right of people accused of crimes to be tried for the alleged crimes within a reasonable amount of time, without arbitrary or indefinite delays. But in many states, this right is rarely enforced with thousands languishing in jails waiting for their cases to be resolved.

Settler Colonialism: Settler colonialism is a type of colonialism where the land and resources of an indigenous peoples are stolen by settlers who permanently form a society there.

The United States was founded as a settler colonial society committed to conquering territory, systematically excluding and eliminating native peoples and enslaving people of African descent for the benefit of White settlers. To this day, the U.S. state denies Indian sovereignty and reparations for slavery and colonization, while it celebrates and maintains the same legal political institutions responsible for dispossession and genocide.

Trial Penalty: The trial penalty refers to the substantial difference between the sentence offered by the prosecutor as part of a plea deal versus the potential sentence imposed if the accused person takes their case to trial. The trial penalty discourages persons accused from going to trial, despite their right to do so, constitutionally.

White Supremacy: "White Supremacy describes a system of power that has its historical roots in the European effort for social, political, economic, and geographical dominance. This system of power is also key to how the U.S. has been organized to systematically benefit white people and act out of violence on people of color."[9]

Notes

Introduction

1. See resources for Abolishing Policing and Abolishing Jailing from Critical Resistance at http://criticalresistance.org/abolish-policing/ and http://criticalresistance.org/abolish-jailing/.
2. "Geographies of Racial Capitalism with Ruth Wilson Gilmore – an Antipode Foundation Film," YouTube, June 1, 2020, https://www.youtube.com/watch?v=2CS627aKrJI.
3. Glossary," The Anti-Violence Project, accessed July 3, 2023, https://www.antiviolenceproject.org/glossary/#ableism.
4. Liat Ben-Moshe, Decarcerating Disability: Deinstitutionalization and Prison Abolition (Minneapolis: University of Minnesota Press, 2022).
5. Harsha Walia and Andrea Smith, Undoing Border Imperialism (Edinburgh: AK Press, 2014).

1. Criminal Courts 101

1. See Chapter Two, "Common Questions About Criminal Court," for more about how "crimes" comes to be defined.
2. Eli Hager, "Where Coronavirus Is Surging—And Electronic Surveillance, Too," *The Marshall Project*, November 22, 2020, https://www.themarshallproject.org/2020/11/22/where-coronavirus-is-surging-and-electronic-surveillance-too.
3. Clark Neily, "Are a Disproportionate Number of Federal Judges Former Government Advocates?," Cato.org, May 27, 2021, https://www.cato.org/study/are-disproportionate-number-federal-judges-former-government-advocates#why-it-matters.
4. "State-Administered Indigent Defense Systems, 2013 ," Bureau of Justice Statistics,

accessed July 3, 2023, https://bjs.ojp.gov/content/pub/pdf/saids13_sum.pdf.

2. Common Questions about Criminal Court Reform

1. Andrea J. Ritchie and Beth E. Richie, *The Crisis Of Criminalization: A Call For A Comprehensive Philanthropic Response* (Barnard Center for Research on Women, 2017), https://bcrw.barnard.edu/wp-content/nfs/reports/NFS9-Challenging-Criminalization-Funding-Perspectives.pdf.

2. "Religious Crimes Code of 1883 Bans Native Dances, Ceremonies," Investing in Native Communities, accessed July 3, 2023, https://nativephilanthropy.candid.org/events/religious-crimes-code-of-1883-bans-native-dances-ceremonies/.

3. Nadra Kareem Nittle, "How the Black Codes Limited African American Progress after the Civil War," History.com, accessed July 3, 2023, https://www.history.com/news/black-codes-reconstruction-slavery.

4. "Jim Crow Laws: Definition, Facts & Timeline," History.com, accessed July 3, 2023, https://www.history.com/topics/early-20th-century-us/jim-crow-laws.

5. "Convict Leasing," *PBS*, accessed July 3, 2023, https://www.pbs.org/tpt/slavery-by-another-name/themes/convict-leasing/.

6. Equal Justice USA. *Racial Inequity and the Death Penalty Past and Present*, n.d. https://ejusa.org/wp-content/uploads/EJUSA-DP-factsheet-race.pdf.

7. Rosich, Katherine J. 2007. *Race, Ethnicity, and the Criminal Justice System*. Washington, DC: American Sociological Association. (Available at http://asanet.org.)

8. Angela Y. Davis, *Abolition Democracy: Beyond Empire Prisons and Torture* (New York, NY: Seven Stories Press, 2005).

9. Rebecca West, "Opera in Greenville," *The New Yorker*, June 6, 1947, https://www.newyorker.com/magazine/1947/06/14/opera-in-greenville.

10. Claudio Saunt, "How Were 1.5 Billion Acres of Land so Rapidly Stolen?," *Aeon*, January 7, 2015, https://aeon.co/essays/how-were-1-5-billion-acres-of-land-so-rapidly-stolen.

11. Kelly Lytle Hernández, "City of Inmates: Conquest, Rebellion and the Rise of Human Caging in Los Angeles (1771-1965)," n.d., https://static1.squarespace.com/static/5a354481a9db0961249f52ec/t/61a6713f1a976a393c1614f8/1638297919393/City+of+Inmates+Zine.pdf.

12. Christopher Klein, "Why Labor Unions Declined in the 1920s," History.com, February 18, 2021, https://www.history.com/news/american-labor-unions-decline-1920s.

13. Christian Gerlach, Clemens Six, and Barbara J. Falk, " The Smith Act Trials and Systemic Violence: Anti-Communist Persecution and Prosecution in America, 1949–1957," essay, in *The Palgrave Handbook of Anti-Communist Persecutions* (Palgrave Macmillan, 2020), 31–49.

14. Alicia J. Campi, "The McCarran-Walter Act: A Contradictory Legacy on Race, Quotas, and Ideology," Immigration Daily, https://www.ilw.com/articles/2004,0708-campi.shtm.

15. Melissa Murray, "MARRIAGE AS PUNISHMENT," *Columbia Law Review* 112, no. 1 (2012): 1–65, http://www.jstor.org/stable/41354748.

16. Mariame Kaba, "Black women punished for self-defense must be freed from their cages," *The Guardian*, January 3, 2019, https://www.theguardian.com/commentisfree/2019/jan/03/cyntoia-brown-marissa-alexander-black-women-self-defense-prison.

17. "Arresting Dress: A Timeline of Anti-Cross-Dressing Laws in the United States," Public Broadcasting Service (PBS), May 31, 2015, https://www.pbs.org/newshour/nation/arresting-dress-timeline-anti-cross-dressing-laws-u-s.

18. "Why Sodomy Laws Matter," ACLU, June 26, 2003, https://www.aclu.org/other/why-sodomy-laws-matter.

19. "2023 anti-trans bills tracker," Trans Legislation Tracker, https://translegislation.com/.

20. Lutz Kaelber, "Oklahoma," Eugenics: Compulsory Sterilization in 50 American States Research Project, 2011, https://www.uvm.edu/~lkaelber/eugenics/OK/OK.html.

21. Shilpa Jindia, "Belly of the Beast: California's dark history of forced sterilizations," *The Guardian*, June 30, 2020, https://www.theguardian.com/us-news/2020/jun/30/california-prisons-forced-sterilizations-belly-beast.

22. The National Institute for Reproductive Health, *When Self-Abortion is a Crime: Laws That Put Women at Risk*, (New York: National Institute for Reproductive Health, 2017),

23. https://www.nirhealth.org/wp-content/uploads/2017/06/Self-Abortion-White-Paper-Final.pdf

24. Nina Luo, *Decriminalizing Survival: Policy Platform And Polling On The Decriminalization Of Sex Work*, Data for Progress, https://www.filesforprogress.org/memos/decriminalizing-sex-work.pdf.

25. Natasha Lennard, "The Supreme Court Will Not Save Us From The Decimation Of Abortion Rights," *The Intercept*, September 1, 2021, https://theintercept.com/2021/09/01/texas-abortion-rights-sb8-supreme-court/

26. Risa Goluboff, *Vagrant Nation: Police Power, Constitutional Change, and the Making of the 1960s*, (Oxford University Press, 2016).

27. Joey L. Mogul, Andrea J. Ritchie, Kay Whitlock, "The Ghosts of Stonewall: Policing Gender, Policing Sex," *Truthout*, July 8, 2015, https://truthout.org/articles/the-ghosts-of-stonewall-policing-gender-policing-sex/.

28. Andrea J. Ritchie, *Invisible No More: Police Violence Against Black Women and Women of Color*, (Beacon University Press, 2017).

29. Bidish Sarma, Jessica Brand, "The Criminalization Of Homelessness: Explained," The Appeal, June 29, 2018, https://theappeal.org/the-criminalization-of-homelessness-an-explainer-aa074d25688d/.

30. Adam Liptak and Glenn Thrush, "Supreme Court Ends Biden's Eviction Moratorium," *The New York Times*, August 26, 2021, https://www.nytimes.com/2021/08/26/us/eviction-moratorium-ends.html.

31. Rachel Reed, "Eviction moratorium's end could cause homelessness or housing insecurity for 'millions of families'," *Harvard Law Today*, July 30, 2021, https://today.law.harvard.edu/eviction-moratoriums-end-could-cause-homelessness-or-housing-insecurity-for-millions-of-families/.

32. Bernadette Rabuy and Daniel Kopf, "Detaining the Poor: How money bail perpetuates an endless cycle of poverty and jail time," *Prison Policy Initiative*, May 10, 2016, https://www.prisonpolicy.org/reports/incomejails.html.

33. Learn more from HEARD at https://behearddc.org.

34. The Sentencing Project, *Report to the United Nations on Racial Disparities in the U.S. Criminal Justice System*, April 19, 2018, https://www.sentencingproject.org/publications/un-report-on-racial-disparities/.

35. Reflective Democracy Campaign, *Tipping The Scales: Challengers Take On The Old Boys' Club Of Elected Prosecutors*, October 2019, https://wholeads.us/research/tipping-the-scales-elected-prosecutors/.

36. Danielle Root, Jake Faleschini, and Grace Oyenubi, *Building a More Inclusive Federal Judiciary*, The Center for American Progress: October 3, 2019, https://www.americanprog-

ress.org/issues/courts/reports/2019/10/03/475359/building-inclusive-federal-judiciary/

37. Malik Neal, "What the Pandemic Revealed About 'Progressive' Prosecutors," *New York Times*, February 4, 2021, https://www.nytimes.com/2021/02/04/opinion/prosecutors-bail-reform.html.

38. Nathan Robinson, "Kamala Harris laughed about jailing parents over truancy. But it's not funny," *The Guardian*, January 31, 2019, https://www.theguardian.com/commentisfree/2019/jan/31/kamala-harris-laughed-jailing-parents-truancy.

39. Read about Liyah's story at https://freeliyah.org/liyahs-story/.

40. Millennial are Killing Capitalism, ""White Reconstruction" - Dylan Rodriguez On Domestic War, The Logics of Genocide, and Abolition," January 7, 2021, https://millennialsarekillingcapitalism.libsyn.com/white-reconstruction-dylan-rodriguez-on-domestic-war-the-logics-of-genocide-and-abolition.

41. Community Justice Exchange and Critical Resistance, *On the Road to Freedom: An Abolitionist Assessment of Pretrial Reforms*, June 2021, https://static1.squarespace.com/static/60db97fe88031352b829d032/t/612d287c0839fa234efb0c3d/1630349448542/RoadToFreedom_Aug2021_FINAL_compressed.pdf.

42. Mariame Kaba and Andrea J. Ritchie, "A World Where George Floyd And Ma'Khia Bryant Would Still Be Here Is A World Without Police," *Newsone*, April 22, 2021, https://newsone.com/4143261/george-floyd-makhia-bryant-abolition-police/.

43. David Sirota, "We're told billionaire tax avoidance is 'perfectly legal'. But is it?," *The Guardian*, June 23, 2021, https://www.theguardian.com/commentisfree/2021/jun/23/billionaire-tax-avoidance-perfectly-legal.

44. Movement 4 Black Lives, "A Progressive Restructuring of All Tax Codes at the Local, State, and Federal Levels to Ensure a Radical and Sustainable Redistribution of Wealth,"

45. file:///Users/rachelforan/Downloads/RestructureTaxCodes-OnePager.pdf.

46. Andrea Guzman, "Lawmakers Love Hate Crime Laws, But Do They Really Protect Anyone?," *Mother Jones*, April 23, 2021, https://www.motherjones.com/crime-justice/2021/04/lawmakers-love-hate-crime-laws-but-do-they-really-protect-anyone/.

47. Bill Chappell, "19-Year-Old Protester Stomped On A 'Back The Blue' Sign. She Faces Hate Crime Charges," *NPR*, July 15, 2021, https://www.npr.org/2021/07/15/1016431004/a-woman-is-facing-a-hate-crime-charge-for-stomping-on-a-back-the-blue-sign-in-ut.

48. "Nassau County Passes Proposal That Would Let Police Sue Protesters," *NBC New York*, August 3, 2021, https://www.nbcnewyork.com/news/local/nassau-county-passes-proposal-that-would-let-police-sue-protesters/3194846/.

49. Elisha Fieldstadt, "Suspect in deadly Atlanta-area spa shootings charged with 8 counts of murder," *NBC News*, March 17, 2021, https://www.nbcnews.com/news/us-news/suspect-deadly-atlanta-area-spa-shootings-says-he-was-motivated-n1261299.

50. Mariame Kaba and Andrea J. Ritchie, "We Want More Justice For Breonna Taylor Than The System That Killed Her Can Deliver," *Essence*, December 6, 2020, https://www.essence.com/feature/breonna-taylor-justice-abolition/.

51. "Criminal Justice Reform Act," New York City Council, https://council.nyc.gov/legislation/criminal-justice-reform/.

52. The Misdemeanor Justice Project of John Jay College of Criminal Justice, *The Criminal Justice Reform Act Evaluation: Post Implementation Changes in Summons Issuance and Outcomes*, September 5, 2018, https://datacollaborativeforjustice.org/wp-content/uploads/2020/04/CJRA-Report-2-1.pdf.

53. Bernard E. Harcourt, An Institutionalization Effect: The Impact of Mental Hospital-

izationand Imprisonment on Homicide in the United States, 1934-2001, 40 J. Legal Stud. 39 (2011).

54. Available at: https://scholarship.law.columbia.edu/faculty_scholarship/2614.

55. Sarah Lazare, "Inside the Endless Nightmare of Indefinite Detention Under 'Civil Commitment'," *In These Times*, August 19, 2020, https://inthesetimes.com/article/civil-commitment-rushville-treatment-detention-facility-prison-indefinite-detention.

56. Mike Maciag, "Addicted to Fines," *Governing*, August 19, 2019, https://www.governing.com/archive/gov-addicted-to-fines.html.

57. Fines & Fees Justice Center, Tip of the Iceberg: How Much Criminal Justice Debt Does the U.S. Really Have?, April 28, 2021, https://finesandfeesjusticecenter.org/2021/04/28/new-ffjc-report-how-much-criminal-justice-debt-does-the-u-s-really-have/.

58. Eli Hager, "Debtors' Prisons, Then and Now: FAQ," *The Marshall Project*, February 24, 2015, https://www.themarshallproject.org/2015/02/24/debtors-prisons-then-and-now-faq.

59. Mariame Kaba and Eva Nagao, *What About the Rapists? An Abolitionist FAQ Series From Interrupting Criminalization*, Interrupting Criminalization: 2021, https://static1.squarespace.com/static/5ee39ec764dbd7179cf1243c/t/6109e65d5a8ce56464f-f94eb/1628038750972/WATR+Zine.pdf.

60. Cassandra Mensah, If We Abolish Police, What Happens to Rapists?," *Teen Vogue*, JUNE 24, 2020, https://www.teenvogue.com/story/what-happens-to-rapists-if-abolish-police.

61. Angel Parker, "What About the Rapists and Murderers?," *Medium*, June 24, 2020, https://medium.com/@amparker/what-about-the-rapists-and-murderers-7a81955b772c.

62. Interrupting Criminalization, "Defund and Domestic Violence Awareness Month," https://static1.squarespace.com/static/5ee39ec764dbd7179cf1243c/t/5f9c405569362b-211c3bcc8d/1604075605257/DEFUND+%26+DVAM.pdf

63. Prison Rape Elimination Act of 2003 (PREA), ACLU, April 29, 2011, https://www.aclu.org/other/prison-rape-elimination-act-2003-prea?redirect=prisoners-rights-womens-rights/prison-rape-elimination-act-2003-prea.

64. James M. Anderson, Maya Buenaventura, and Paul S. Heaton, The Effects of Holistic Defense on Criminal Justice Outcomes (2019), Harvard Law Review, Vol. 132, p. 819, 2019, U of Penn, Inst for Law & Econ Research Paper No. 18-33, Available at SSRN: https://ssrn.com/abstract=3284042.

65. Community Justice Exchange, *Transparency is Not Enough: A Framework for Building Campaign Strategy*, https://static1.squarespace.com/static/60db97fe88031352b829d032/t/60d-cd93afd55084e0cd806c1/1625086271897/CJE_TransparencyFramework_Final.pdf

66. Community Justice Exchange, *From Data Criminalization to Prison Abolition*, https://abolishdatacrim.org/en/report/introduction.

67. Community Justice Exchange, *An Organizer's Guide to Confronting Pretrial Risk Assessment Tools in Decarceration Campaigns*, December 2019, https://static1.squarespace.com/static/60db97fe88031352b829d032/t/60dcd6e6ac9dae69c2243313/1625085675244/CJE_PretrialRATGuide_FinalDec2019Version.pdf.

68. Youth Justice Center, "About the Space," https://youthjusticela.org/about-the-space/.

69. "Juvenile justice center scheduled for return to South Los Angeles," *Our Weekly LA*, March 29, 2018, https://ourweekly.com/news/2018/03/29/juvenile-justice-center-scheduled-return-south-los/.

70. Community Justice Exchange and Critical Resistance, *On The Road To Freedom: An Abolitionist Assessment of Pretrial and Bail Reforms*, June 2021, https://static1.squarespace.

com/static/60db97fe88031352b829d032/t/612d287c0839fa234efb0c3d/1630349448542/
RoadToFreedom_Aug2021_FINAL_compressed.pdf.

71. Critical Resistance, *The CR Abolition Organizing Toolkit*, 2004, https://criticalresistance.
org/wp-content/uploads/2020/05/CR-Abolitionist-Toolkit-online.pdf, pg 65.

3. Problem-Creating Courts

1. Miller, Reuben Jonathan. "Devolving the Carceral State: Race, Prisoner Reentry, and the
Micro-Politics of Urban Poverty Management." *Punishment & Society* 16, no. 3 (2014):
305–35. https://doi.org/10.1177/1462474514527487.

2. Ritchie, Andrea J., and Jared Knowles . "Cops Don't Stop Violence." Interrupting Criminalization . Accessed June 22, 2022. https://static1.squarespace.com/
static/5ee39ec764dbd7179cf1243c/t/60ff3d8f0a0ef6473fbb6dbb/1627340186125/
Cops+Don%27t+Stop+Violence; Richie, Beth E. and Andrea J. Ritchie, *The Crisis of Criminalization: A Call for A Comprehensive Response*, Interrupting Criminalization (2017).

3. "Frequently Asked Questions." *Beyond Criminal Courts*. Accessed June 22, 2022. https://
beyondcourts.org/en/learn/faq.

4. Lowry, Michela, and Ashmini Kerodal. "Prosecutor Led Diversion: A National Survey,"
March 2019. https://www.courtinnovation.org/sites/default/files/media/document/2019/
prosecutor-led_diversion.pdf.

5. Collins, Erin R. "The Problem of Problem-Solving Courts." U.C. Davis Law Review 54
(November 22, 2019): 1573–1629. https://doi.org/10.2139/ssrn.3492003.

6. Andrea J. Ritchie and Black Lives Matter Chicago, *Epicenter Chicago: Reclaiming a City
from Neoliberalism*, Political Research Associates (2019); Metcalf, Stephen. "Neoliberalism: The Idea That Swallowed the World." *The Guardian*. Guardian News and Media,
August 18, 2017. https://www.theguardian.com/news/2017/aug/18/neoliberalism-the-
idea-that-changed-the-world.

7. Goodman, Amy. "The Case for Prison Abolition: Ruth Wilson Gilmore on COVID-19,
Racial Capitalism & Decarceration." Democracy Now!, May 5, 2020. https://www.de-
mocracynow.org/2020/5/5/ruth_wilson_gilmore_abolition_coronavirus.

8. Gilmore, Ruth Wilson. "The Problem with Innocence." *Inquest*, May 12, 2022. https://
inquest.org/ruth-wilson-gilmore-the-problem-with-innocence/.

9. Story, Brett. *Prison Land: Mapping Carceral Power Across Neoliberal America*. Minneapolis,
MN: University of Minnesota Press, 2019.

10. This is to say nothing of the fact that many people spend time in jail prior to their
diversion. In a sense, almost everyone in diversion spends some time incarcerated,
even if "just" during booking and waiting for arraignment. Wang, Leah, and Katie Rose
Quandt. "Building Exits off the Highway to Mass Incarceration: Diversion Programs
Explained." Prison Policy Initiative, July 20, 2021. https://www.prisonpolicy.org/reports/
diversion.html.

11. Eisenberg-Guyot, Nadja (2022). "Refusing Rehabilitation: Outlaw Epistemologies and
the Carceral-Therapeutic State in NYC." [Doctoral Dissertation, Graduate Center of
the City University of New York]. ProQuest Dissertations Publishing; Fields, Barbara
J. "The Heartless Paternalism of the Slaveholder." The Washington Post, August 29,
1982. https://www.washingtonpost.com/archive/entertainment/books/1982/08/29/
the-heartless-paternalism-of-the-slaveholder/6cb8ca39-0efa-4861-913c-bfe5df9d38e5/.

12. The paternalistic logic undergirding many traditional court dynamics is taken to even
bigger extremes in diversion court settings, and has its direct roots in the slavery and

colonization that the United States was founded on.

13. Cohen, Stanley. "The Punitive City: Notes on the Dispersal of Social Control." Contemporary Crises 3, no. 4 (October 1979): 339–63. https://doi.org/10.1007/bf00729115.

14. Gottschalk, Marie. "Raze the Carceral State." *Dissent Magazine*, November 24, 2015. https://www.dissentmagazine.org/article/criminal-justice-reform-minimum-sentencing-mass-incarceration.

15. Collins, Erin R. "The Problem of Problem-Solving Courts." *U.C. Davis Law Review* 54 (November 22, 2019): 1573–1629. https://doi.org/10.2139/ssrn.3492003.

16. Most, if not all, drug courts and mental health courts task judges with making medical decisions as a fact of their existence and routine operation. Boldt, Richard C. "Rehabilitative Punishment and the Drug Treatment Court Movement." *Washington University Law Quarterly* 76, no. 4 (1998): 1205–1306; McCoy, Candace, Wolf Heydebrand, and Rekha Mirchandani. "The Problem With Problem-Solving Justice: Coercion vs. Democratic Deliberation." *Restorative Justice* 3, no. 2 (October 14, 2015): 159–87. https://doi.org/10.1080/20504721.2015.1069085. For one specific example of a drug court in Massachusetts, see Herz, Mark. "Mass. Drug Courts Settle with US Attorney's Office over Interfering with Treatment." GBH, March 25, 2022. https://www.wgbh.org/news/local-news/2022/03/25/mass-drug-courts-settle-with-us-attorneys-office-over-interfering-with-treatment.

17. Kilgore, James. "Repackaging Mass Incarceration." Prison Legal News, November 8, 2014. https://www.prisonlegalnews.org/news/2014/nov/8/repackaging-mass-incarceration/.

18. Pishko, Jessica. "How a Criminal Justice Reform Became an Enrichment Scheme." Pulitzer Center, July 15, 2019. https://pulitzercenter.org/stories/how-criminal-justice-reform-became-enrichment-scheme; "No Such Thing as 'Progressive Prosecutors.'" *Beyond Criminal Courts*. Accessed June 22, 2022. https://beyondcourts.org/en/learn/no-such-thing-progressive-prosecutors.

19. Andrea J. Ritchie and Black Lives Matter Chicago, *Epicenter Chicago: Reclaiming a City from Neoliberalism*, Political Research Associates (2019).

20. Collins, Erin R. "The Problem of Problem-Solving Courts." *UC Davis Law Review* 54 (November 22, 2019): 1573–1629. https://doi.org/10.2139/ssrn.3492003.

21. Tiger, Rebecca. "Drug Courts and the Logic of Coerced Treatment." *Sociological Forum* 26, no. 1 (2011): 169–82. https://doi.org/10.1111/j.1573-7861.2010.01229.x.

22. Eisenberg-Guyot, Nadja (2022). "Refusing Rehabilitation: Outlaw Epistemologies and the Carceral-Therapeutic State in NYC." [Doctoral Dissertation, Graduate Center of the City University of New York]. ProQuest Dissertations Publishing.

23. "Advancing Public Health Interventions to Address the Harms of the Carceral System." American Public Health Association, October 26, 2021. https://www.apha.org/Policies-and-Advocacy/Public-Health-Policy-Statements/Policy-Database/2022/01/07/Advancing-Public-Health-Interventions-to-Address-the-Harms-of-the-Carceral-System.

24. Braveman, P., & Gottlieb, L. (2014). The Social Determinants of Health: It's Time to Consider the Causes of the Causes. Public Health Reports, 129(2), 19–31. https://doi.org/10.1177/00333549141291s206

25. Cohen, Stanley. "The Punitive City: Notes on the Dispersal of Social Control." *Contemporary Crises* 3, no. 4 (October 1979): 339–63. https://doi.org/10.1007/bf00729115.

26. David S. Festinger et al., "Expungement of Arrest Records in Drug Court: Do Clients Know What They're Missing?," *Drug Court Review* 5, no. 1 (2005).

27. Collins, Erin, *The Problem of Problem-Solving Courts* (November 22, 2019). *UC Davis Law*

Review, Vol. 54, No. 1573, 2021, Available at SSRN: https://ssrn.com/abstract=3492003 or http://dx.doi.org/10.2139/ssrn.3492003

4. Community Interventions to Shift Power

28. Mariame Kaba, "Free Us All: Participatory defense campaigns as abolitionist organizing," *The New Inquiry*, May 8, 2017, https://thenewinquiry.com/free-us-all/.

29. Jocelyn Simonson, "What is Community Justice?", *n+1*, July 19, 2017, https://www.nplusonemag.com/online-only/online-only/what-is-community-justice/

30. Learn more about Justice Committee's work at https://www.justicecommittee.org/cop-watch.

31. Check out the Berkley Copwatch and WITNESS People's Database at https://www.berkeleycopwatch.org/people-s-database.

32. Court Watch NYC, "Breaking Down the New York City Punishment Machine," https://static1.squarespace.com/static/5a21b2c1b1ffb67b3f4b2d16/t/611d6293b70904730ab70496/1629315731303/aug+2021_Courtwatch_Zine.pdf

33. The Coalition to End Money Bond, "Monitoring Cook County's Central Bond Court A Community Courtwatching Initiative," February 27, 2018, https://chicagobond.org/wp-content/uploads/2018/10/courtwatching-report_coalition-to-end-money-bond-final_2-25-18.pdf.

34. Learn more about Baltimore Court Watch at https://baltimorecourtwatch.org.

35. Learn more about the Chicago Community Bond Fund at https://chicagobond.org/advocacy/.

36. See the National Bail Fund Network's Directory of bail funds at https://www.communityjusticeexchange.org/en/nbfn-directory.

37. Coalition to End Money Bond, "Governor Pritzker To Sign The Pretrial Fairness Act & Officially Ends Money Bond In Illinois!," https://endmoneybond.org/2021/02/22/governor-pritzker-to-sign-the-pretrial-fairness-act-officially-end-money-bond-in-illinois/.

38. Learn more about the National Bail Out collective at https://www.nationalbailout.org.

39. Learn more about the campaign to close the jail in Atlanta at https://www.closethejailatl.org.

40. Gabrielle Hernandez, "How Southern organizers are leading the movement to end money bail," *Scalawag*, https://scalawagmagazine.org/2018/05/how-southern-organizers-are-leading-the-movement-to-end-money-bail/

41. Learn more about Nashville Participatory Defense Hub at https://www.facebook.com/615ParticipatoryDefense/.

42. Learn more about the National Participatory Defense Network at https://www.participatorydefense.org/hubs.

43. Learn more about Free Hearts at https://www.freeheartsorg.com/about.

44. Learn more about the #FreeBesha Defense Campaign at https://freebresha.wordpress.com/2018/02/06/bresha-meadows-returns-home-after-collective-organizing-efforts/.

45. Learn more about Survived and Punished at https://survivedandpunished.org.

46. United States v. Moylan, 417 F. 2d 1002 (1969).

47. Benjamin Weiser, "Jury Statute Not Violated by Protester, Judge Rules," *New York Times*, April 19, 2012, https://www.nytimes.com/2012/04/20/nyregion/indictment-against-julian-heicklen-jury-nullification-advocate-is-dismissed.html.

48. John Tunison, "Man handing out pamphlets outside West Michigan courthouse cleared of jury tampering," *MLive*, July 28, 2020, https://www.9and10news.com/2020/07/28/

michigan-supreme-court-overturns-mecosta-co-jury-tampering-conviction/.

49. German Lopez, "Jury nullification: how jurors can stop unfair and racist laws in the courtroom," *Vox*, May 2, 2016, https://www.vox.com/2016/5/2/11538752/jury-nullification-paul-butler.

50. Doug McConnell, "A Juror's Guide to Going Rogue," *Practical Ethics*, May 14, 2021, http://blog.practicalethics.ox.ac.uk/2021/05/a-jurors-guide-to-going-rogue/.

5. Defunding Courts

1. Project NIA, "Defund Police," YouTube, https://www.youtube.com/watch?v=bT0YpOmk8NA.

2. War Resisters League, "War Tax Resistance," https://www.warresisters.org/war-tax-resistance.

3. Learn more about police abolition campaigns at http://defundpolice.org.

4. Brendan Roediger, Abolish Municipal Courts: A Response to Professor Natapoff (February 20, 2021). *Harvard Law Review*, Vol. 134, No. F, p. 213, 2021, Saint Louis U. Legal Studies Research Paper No. 2021-08, Available at SSRN: https://ssrn.com/abstract=3797207

5. Matthew Clair and Amanda Woog, Courts and the Abolition Movement (February 13, 2021). *California Law Review*, Vol. 110, No. 1, 2022, Available at SSRN: https://papers.ssrn.com/sol3/papers.cfm?abstract_id=3785373.

6. Wendy Sawyer and Peter Wagner, "Mass Incarceration: The Whole Pie 2022," *Prison Policy Initiative*, March 14, 2022, https://www.prisonpolicy.org/reports/pie2022.html.

7. Court Statistics Project, "CSP STAT Criminal," https://www.courtstatistics.org/csp-stat-nav-cards-first-row/csp-stat-criminal.

8. Simone Seiver, "A Millennial's Guide to 'Broken Windows'," *The Marshall Project*, May 20, 2015, https://www.themarshallproject.org/2015/05/20/a-millennial-s-guide-to-broken-windows?gclid=CjwKCAjwzeqVBhAoEiwAOrEmzSPLJn5r5cgxy2PsHFaIrx-7WrJciESVch5YlppWEDee870pQBx7dhoCpAAQAvD_BwE

9. John F. Pfaff, *The Causes of Growth in Prison Admissions and Populations* (January 23, 2012). Available at SSRN: https://ssrn.com/abstract=1990508 or http://dx.doi.org/10.2139/ssrn.1990508

10. Community Resource Hub and Interrupting Criminalization, *Cops Don't Stop Violence: Combatting Narratives Used to Defend Police Instead of Defund Them*, https://communityresourcehub.org/wp-content/uploads/2021/07/0726_PoliceDontStop_C.pdf.

11. Erwin Chemerinsky, *Presumed Guilty: How the Supreme Court Empowered the Police and Subverted Civil Rights* (Liveright, 2021).

12. National Police Accountability Project, "Learn about the effects of absolute immunity for prosecutors," https://www.nlg-npap.org/absolute-immunity/.

13. Barry Friedman, Why Do Courts Defer to Cops?, 130 Harv. L. Rev. F. 323, https://harvardlawreview.org/2017/06/why-do-courts-defer-to-cops/.

14. Joseph Goldstein, "'Testilying' by Police: A Stubborn Problem," *New York Times*, March 18, 2018, https://www.nytimes.com/2018/03/18/nyregion/testilying-police-perjury-new-york.html.

15. The Center for Popular Democracy, Law for Black Lives, and Black Youth Project 100, *Freedom to Thrive: Reimagining Safety & Security in our Communities*, https://populardemocracy.org/sites/default/files/Freedom%20To%20Thrive%2C%20Higher%20Res%20Version.pdf.

16. Vera Institute of Justice, "Time Line," September 2014, https://www.vera.org/justice-in-

focus-crime-bill-20/time-line.

17. Isaac Shapiro, Bryann Dasilva, David Reich And Richard Kogan, *Funding for Housing, Health, and Social Services Block Grants Has Fallen Markedly Over Time*, Center on Budget and and Policy Priorities: March 24, 2016, https://www.cbpp.org/research/federal-budget/funding-for-housing-health-and-social-services-block-grants-has-fallen.

18. Marquisha Johns and Jill Rosenthal, *How Investing in Public Health Will Strengthen America's Health*, Center for American Progress: May 17, 2022, https://www.americanprogress.org/article/how-investing-in-public-health-will-strengthen-americas-health/.

19. Steven Jessen-Howard, Rasheed Malik, and MK Falgout, *Costly and Unavailable: America Lacks Sufficient Child Care Supply for Infants and Toddlers*, Center for American Progress: August 4, 2020, https://www.americanprogress.org/article/costly-unavailable-america-lacks-sufficient-child-care-supply-infants-toddlers/.

20. The Century Foundation, *Closing America's Education Funding Gaps*, July 22, 2020, https://tcf.org/content/report/closing-americas-education-funding/.

21. Center on Budget and Policy Priorities, "Policy Basics: Public Housing," June 16, 2021, https://www.cbpp.org/research/public-housing.

22. Learn more about Black Nashville Assembly at https://www.blacknashvilleassembly.org/.

23. Angélica Cházaro, Erica Perry, and Andrea Ritchie, moderated by Dean Spade, "Abolition on the Ground: Reporting from the Movement to #DefundthePolice," (online panel discussion, Barnard Center for Research on Women, March 1, 2022), https://bcrw.barnard.edu/event/abolition-on-the-ground-reporting-from-the-movement-to-defundthepolice/.

24. Learn more about the Seattle Solidarity Budget coalition at https://www.seattlesolidaritybudget.com/.

25. Angélica Cházaro, Erica Perry, and Andrea Ritchie, moderated by Dean Spade, "Abolition on the Ground: Reporting from the Movement to #DefundthePolice," (online panel discussion, Barnard Center for Research on Women, March 1, 2022), https://bcrw.barnard.edu/event/abolition-on-the-ground-reporting-from-the-movement-to-defundthepolice/.

26. Seattle Solidarity Budget, "Solidarity Budget: A Call to Action for 2021 Budget and Beyond," https://docs.google.com/document/d/1meeXTETSLaZEwdS9Ec2SF1_aT-ZOKs1JJhArY3J3wDvU/edit#heading=h.4gnsac3q3dw3.

27. See the budget proposal at https://www.seattlesolidaritybudget.com/.

28. Detention Watch Network, *Communities Not Cages: A Just Transition from Immigrant Detention Economies*, 2021, https://www.detentionwatchnetwork.org/sites/default/files/reports/Communities%20Not%20Cages-A%20Just%20Transition%20from%20Immigration%20Detention%20Economies_DWN%202021.pdf.

29. To check out this tool visit https://defundpolice.org/budgeting-tools/for-spending-and-personnel-over-time/.

6. No Such Thing As Progressive Prosecutors

30. Community Justice Exchange, Court Watch MA, Families for Justice as Healing, Project NIA, and Survived and Punished NY, *Abolitionist Principles & Campaign Strategies For Prosecutor Organizing*, 2019, https://www.communityjusticeexchange.org/en/abolitionist-principles.

31. More resources on the misnomer of "progressive prosecutors": Rachel Foran, Mariame Kaba, Katy Naples-Mitchell, "Abolitionist Principles for Prosecutor Organizing:

Origins and Next Steps," 16 Stan. J. C.R. & C.L. 496 (2021); Benjamin Levin, "Imagining the Progressive Prosecutor," 105 Minnesota Law Review 1415 (2021); "The Paradox of 'Progressive Prosecution,'" 132 Harv. L. Rev. 748, 752 (2018); Survived & Punished NY, "No Good Prosecutors Now or Ever" (June 2021); Gyasi Lake, "There's no such thing as a 'progressive prosecutor' in a system designed to criminalize Blackness," Black Youth Project (July 10, 2019); Ephrat Livni, "The problem with Tiffany Cabán and the new cult of 'progressive prosecutors,'" Quartz (June 28, 2019).

32. Benjamin Levin, "Imagining the Progressive Prosecutor," 105 *Minnesota Law Review* 1415 (2021), https://minnesotalawreview.org/wp-content/uploads/2021/02/Levin_MLR.pdf

33. Daniel A Medina, "The progressive prosecutors blazing a new path for the US justice system," *The Guardian*, July 23, 2019, https://www.theguardian.com/us-news/2019/jul/23/us-justice-system-progressive-prosecutors-mass-incarceration-death-penalty.

34. "Reimagining Prosecution: Progress and Resistance," Vera Institute of Justice, https://www.vera.org/events/reimagining-prosecution-progress-and-resistance.

35. Emily Bazelon, *Charged: The New Movement to Transform American Prosecution and End Mass Incarceration*, (New York: Random House, 2019).

36. Harry Cheadle, "Meet the Mega-donors Behind the Push for Progressive Prosecutors," Blue Tent, https://bluetent.us/articles/campaigns-elections/who/.

37. "Progressive prosecutors scored big wins in 2020 elections, boosting a nationwide trend," The Conversation, November 18, 2020, https://theconversation.com/progressive-prosecutors-scored-big-wins-in-2020-elections-boosting-a-nationwide-trend-149322.

38. Rachael S. Rollins, *Holding Prosecutor Offices Accountable: The Suffolk County District Attorney's Office's Approach to Progressive Prosecution*, 16 Stan. J. C.R. & C.L. 564 (2021)

39. "Meet the Movement," Fair and Just Prosecution, https://fairandjustprosecution.org/meet-the-movement/.

40. Andrea Estes, "Suffolk DA Rollins Moving Away High Cash Bail Hold Potentially Dangerous Defendants," *The Boston Globe*, August 25, 2020, https://www.bostonglobe.com/2020/08/25/metro/suffolk-da-rollins-moving-away-high-cash-bail-hold-potentially-dangerous-defendants/.

41. Mensah M. Dean and Chris Palmer, "Amid rising gun crime in Philly, Da Larry Krasner blasts low bail," *The Philadelphia Inquirer*, January 11, 2021, "https://www.inquirer.com/news/larry-krasner-homicide-police-department-district-attorney--20210112.html

42. Malik Neal, "What the Pandemic Revealed About 'Progressive' Prosecutors," *New York Times*, February 4, 2021, https://www.nytimes.com/2021/02/04/opinion/prosecutors-bail-reform.html.

43. "Krasner fights impending $8.7M budget cut to DA's Office," *Pennsylvania Capital Star*, June 9, 2020, https://www.penncapital-star.com/criminal-justice/krasner-fights-impending-8-7m-budget-cut-to-das-office/#:~:text=Krasner%20pleaded%20with%20members%20of,his%20%244.9%20billion%20spending%20plan.

44. The Council of the City of New York, *Report of the Finance Division on the Fiscal 2021-2024 Preliminary Financial Plan For the District Attorneys and Office of Special Narcotics Prosecutor*, March 19, 2020,

45. https://council.nyc.gov/budget/wp-content/uploads/sites/54/2020/03/901-906-DA-and-SNP.pdf.

46. Suffolk District Attorney's Office Budget Summary, https://budget.digital.mass.gov/summary/fy21/enacted/independents/district-attorneys/suffolk-da?tab=historical-budget.

47. Roy Hanna, "Is Baltimore State's Attorney Marilyn Mosby too distracted to fulfill her duties? These statistics suggest she is," *The Baltimore Sun*, June 16, 2021, https://www.baltimoresun.com/opinion/op-ed/bs-ed-op-0617-mosby-prosecution-20210616-hxptnsdkfzeardgoynx7bdedja-story.html.

48. "Krasner fights impending $8.7M budget cut to DA's Office," *Pennsylvania Capital Star*, June 9, 2020, https://www.penncapital-star.com/criminal-justice/krasner-fights-impending-8-7m-budget-cut-to-das-office/#:~:text=Krasner%20pleaded%20with%20members%20of,his%20%244.9%20billion%20spending%20plan.

49. Arnold Ventures, "District Attorney Krasner Announces DAO Transparency & Accountability Research Collaboration," March 11, 2020, https://www.arnoldventures.org/newsroom/district-attorney-krasner-announces-dao-transparency-accountability-research-collaboration.

50. Chan Zuckerberg Initiative, "Transforming Prosecution," November 22, 2019, https://chanzuckerberg.com/newsroom/transforming-prosecution/.

51. Fair and Justice Prosecution, https://fairandjustprosecution.org.

52. Benjamin Schneider, Is San Francisco Re-Funding the Police?," *SFWeekly*, June 16, 2021, https://www.sfweekly.com/news/is-san-francisco-re-funding-the-police/.

53. District Attorney Kings County, "Brooklyn District Attorney Eric Gonzalez Announces Project Reset in Partnership with the Center for Court Innovation and the Brooklyn Museum To Allow Those Arrested for Certain Minor Offenses to Avoid Prosecution," October 2, 2019, http://www.brooklynda.org/2019/10/02/brooklyn-district-attorney-eric-gonzalez-announces-project-reset-in-partnership-with-the-center-for-court-innovation-and-the-brooklyn-museum-to-allow-those-arrested-for-certain-minor-offenses-to-avoid/.

54. Philadelphia DAO, "DA Krasner Announces First Round of Violence Prevention Grant Awards to Community-Based Groups," May 10, 2021, https://medium.com/philadelphia-justice/da-krasner-announces-first-round-of-violence-prevention-grant-awards-to-community-based-groups-ef0e0190e4f9.

55. Suffolk County District Attorney Massachusetts, "Community Reinvestment Grants," https://www.suffolkdistrictattorney.com/community-reinvestment-grant.

56. "Why Restorative Justice Should Be on Every Prosecutor's To-Do List," *The Crime Report*, May 1, 2019, https://thecrimereport.org/2019/05/01/why-restorative-justice-should-be-on-every-prosecutors-to-do-list/?fbclid=IwAR2cxisU2KYsDRxTqRuhkhPB-DGH_icLzIyI-FrHz3nRbjo8SKHltxRADuI.

57. San Francisco District Attorney, "Partnership with Lyft to Provide Rides to Victims of DV," https://sfdistrictattorney.org/press-release/partnership-with-lyft-to-provide-rides-to-victims-of-dv/.

58. San Francisco District Attorney, "Da Boudin Partners with Newsom and Airbnb to Support Survivors," https://sfdistrictattorney.org/press-release/da-boudin-partners-with-newsom-and-airbnb-to-support-dv-survivors/.

59. Elias Rodriques, Melonie Griffiths, and Ralowe Ampu, "Prosecutors Have No Place in Truth, Justice and Reconciliation Commissions, *Truthout*, August 22, 2020, https://truthout.org/articles/prosecutors-have-no-place-in-truth-justice-and-reconciliation-commissions/

60. Ron Cassie, "The Many Trials of Keith Davis Jr.," *Baltimore*, November 2021, https://www.baltimoremagazine.com/section/historypolitics/the-many-trials-of-keith-davis-jr-remains-incarcerated-wife-fights-for-his-freedom/.

61. "Philly DA Larry Krasner: Trump Is a "Wannabe Fascist." I Will Charge His Agents If They Break Law," *Democracy Now*, July 23, 2020, https://www.democracynow.org/2020/7/23/larry_krasner_philadelphia_protests_federal_agents.

62. Suffolk County District Attorney Massachusettshttps, "Suffolk DA Rachael Rollins Statement on Bail and the Bail Fund," August 11, 2020, https://www.suffolkdistrictattorney.com/press-releases/items/bail-fund.

63. Jeremy B. White, "California prosecutors revolt against Los Angeles DA's social justice changes," *Politico*, https://www.politico.com/news/2021/01/25/george-gascon-california-social-justice-461667.

64. Tom Jackman, "Arlington prosecutor goes to Va. Supreme Court against judges who challenge her new policies," *Washington Post*, August 28, 2020, https://www.washingtonpost.com/dc-md-va/2020/08/28/arlington-prosecutor-goes-va-supreme-court-against-judges-who-challenge-her-new-policies/.

65. Keri Blakinger, "Prosecutors Who Want to Curb Mass Incarceration Hit a Roadblock: Tough-on-Crime Lawmakers," *The Marshall Project*, February 3, 2022, https://www.themarshallproject.org/2022/02/03/prosecutors-who-want-to-curb-mass-incarceration-hit-a-roadblock-tough-on-crime-lawmakers.

66. Jonah Bromwich, "Manhattan D.A. Sharpens Crime Policies That Led to Weeks of Backlash," *New York Times*, February 4, 2022, https://www.nytimes.com/2022/02/04/nyregion/manhattan-da-alvin-bragg-memo-prosecution.html.

67. "Aramis Ayala yanked from case by second GOP governor, this time DeSantis," *Tampa Bay Times*, January 31, 2020, https://www.tampabay.com/florida-politics/buzz/2020/01/31/aramis-ayala-yanked-from-case-by-second-gop-governor-this-time-desantis/.

68. Rashad Robinson, "The People Who Undermine Progressive Prosecutors," *New York Times*, June 11, 2020, https://www.nytimes.com/2020/06/11/opinion/george-floyd-prosecutors.html.

69. <?> Mariame Kaba and Andrea J. Ritchie, "We Want More Justice For Breonna Taylor Than The System That Killed Her Can Deliver," *Essence*, December 6, 2020 https://www.essence.com/feature/breonna-taylor-justice-abolition/.

7. Abolitionist Principles & Campaign Strategies for Prosecutor Organizing

1. This definition of Mutual Aid comes from Big Door Brigade. Learn more here: http://bigdoorbrigade.com/what-is-mutual-aid/.

2. Raj Jayadev & Pilar Weiss, "Organizing Towards a New Vision of Community Justice," *Law & Political Economy Blog*, May 9, 2019, https://lpeblog.org/2019/05/09/organizing-towards-a-new-vision-of-community-justice/.

Glossary

1. Glossary," The Anti-Violence Project, accessed July 3, 2023, https://www.antiviolenceproject.org/glossary/#ableism.

2. Liat Ben-Moshe, *Decarcerating Disability: Deinstitutionalization and Prison Abolition* (Minneapolis: University of Minnesota Press, 2022).

3. Harsha Walia and Andrea Smith, *Undoing Border Imperialism* (Edinburgh: AK Press, 2014).

4. Clark Neily, "Are a Disproportionate Number of Federal Judges Former Government

Advocates?," Cato.org, May 27, 2021, https://www.cato.org/study/are-disproportion-ate-number-federal-judges-former-government-advocates#why-it-matters.

5. David S. Festinger et al., "Expungement of Arrest Records in Drug Court: Do Clients Know What They're Missing?," *Drug Court Review* 5, no. 1 (2005).

6. Collins, Erin, The Problem of Problem-Solving Courts (November 22, 2019). *UC Davis Law Review*, Vol. 54, No. 1573, 2021, Available at SSRN: https://ssrn.com/abstract=3492003 or http://dx.doi.org/10.2139/ssrn.3492003

7. "State-Administered Indigent Defense Systems, 2013 ," Bureau of Justice Statistics, accessed July 3, 2023, https://bjs.ojp.gov/content/pub/pdf/saids13_sum.pdf.

8. "Geographies of Racial Capitalism with Ruth Wilson Gilmore – an Antipode Foundation Film," YouTube, June 1, 2020, https://www.youtube.com/watch?v=2CS627aKrJI.

9. Critical Resistance, *The CR Abolition Organizing Toolkit*, 2004, https://criticalresistance.org/wp-content/uploads/2020/05/CR-Abolitionist-Toolkit-online.pdf, pg 65.

Acknowledgments

Unless otherwise noted, each resource re-published as a chapter in this book was written by Rachel Foran and Zohra Ahmed, in collaboration with Andrea J. Ritchie, Mariame Kaba, and Woods Ervin. Unless otherwise noted, the resources were originally published in July 2022 with the launch of the beyondcourts.org website.

We are grateful to be in struggle and community with brilliant people who provided critical feedback on different resources contained in this book: Amna Akbar, Emmanuel Andre, Monica Cosby, Premal Dharia, Sharlyn Grace, Savannah Felix, Eli Hadley, Andrea James, Katy Naples Mitchell, Atara Rich-Shea, Catherine Sevcenko, Jocelyn Simonson, Pilar Weiss, Amanda Woog, and Nathan Yaffe. Thanks to the law students who provided research and notetaking support: Jacob Friedman, Hailey Laurie, Charlie McKeown, and Millie Price.

The original website (beyondcourts.org) where this material was first published was built by Research Action Design. Illustrations by Noah Jodice. Web design support from C4 Tech & Design.

To turn the website into this book, thanks to Noah Jodice for layout design and to Eli Hadley for proofreading and feedback.

Below are the acknowledgements and authorship for resources included in this collection that were written and reviewed by others:

"Problem Creating Courts" was developed by Rachel Foran and Eli Hadley, in conversation with Zohra Ahmed, Emmanuel Andre, Monica Cosby, Premal Dharia, Savannah Felix, Sharlyn Grace, Katy Naples-Mitchell, Jocelyn Simonson, and Amanda Woog. Sincere thanks to Millie Price for extensive research and citations support. Thanks to Puck Lo, Christine Mitchell from the End Police Violence Collective, Aliza Cohen and Allie Mikolanis from Drug Policy Alliance, Nadja Eisenberg-Guyot, and Andrea J. Ritchie for reviewing and providing critical feedback.

"Abolitionist Principles and Campaign Strategies for Prosecutor Organizing" was developed in 2019 by the following organizations: Community Justice Exchange, CourtWatch MA, Families for Justice as Healing, Project NIA, and Survived and Punished NY. Thanks to Fahd Ahmed, Amna Akbar, Erin Miles Cloud, Lily Fahsi-Haskell, Ruth Wilson Gilmore, Craig Gilmore, Joey Mogul, Andrea Ritchie, Lisa Sangoi, Dean Spade and others for reviewing and providing critical feedback.

About Haymarket Books

Haymarket Books is a radical, independent, nonprofit book publisher based in Chicago. Our mission is to publish books that contribute to struggles for social and economic justice. We strive to make our books a vibrant and organic part of social movements and the education and development of a critical, engaged, and internationalist Left.

We take inspiration and courage from our namesakes, the Haymarket Martyrs, who gave their lives fighting for a better world. Their 1886 struggle for the eight-hour day—which gave us May Day, the international workers' holiday—reminds workers around the world that ordinary people can organize and struggle for their own liberation. These struggles—against oppression, exploitation, environmental devastation, and war—continue today across the globe.

Since our founding in 2001, Haymarket has published more than nine hundred titles. Radically independent, we seek to drive a wedge into the risk-averse world of corporate book publishing. Our authors include Angela Y. Davis, Arundhati Roy, Keeanga-Yamahtta Taylor, Eve Ewing, Aja Monet, Mariame Kaba, Naomi Klein, Rebecca Solnit, Olúfémi O. Táíwò, Mohammed El-Kurd, José Olivarez, Noam Chomsky, Winona LaDuke, Robyn Maynard, Leanne Betasamosake Simpson, Howard Zinn, Mike Davis, Marc Lamont Hill, Dave Zirin, Astra Taylor, and Amy Goodman, among many other leading writers of our time. We are also the trade publishers of the acclaimed Historical Materialism Book Series.

Haymarket also manages a vibrant community organizing and event space in Chicago, Haymarket House, the popular Haymarket Books Live event series and podcast, and the annual Socialism Conference.